Care and Breeding of

Panther, Jackson's, Veiled, and Parson's Chameleons

Edited by
Philippe de Vosjoli
Gary Ferguson

The Herpetocultural Library

Advanced
Vivarium
Systems, inc.

10728 Prospect Ave. Suite G
Santee, CA 92071-4558 USA

Library of Congress Catalog Card Number: 96–183295

ISBN 1-882770307

PRINTED AND BOUND IN THE UNITED STATES OF AMERICA.

Cover photography by Bill Love and Andra Indriksone.
Design and layout by Bridget M. Pilcher.

Contents

Part I

Panther Chameleon
(Chamaeleo pardalis)
Natural History, Captive Management and Breeding

Co-authored by
Gary Ferguson
James B. Murphy
Achille Raselemananana
Jean-Baptiste Ramananmanjato

Introduction and Natural History

The panther chameleon is a medium-large, highly sexually dimorphic, and often spectacularly colored Malagasy species. The larger (up to 22 inches or 55.9 cm in total length) males vary geographically in color and head ornamentation, while the smaller (up to 13 inches or 33 cm) females are more uniform throughout their range (Brygoo 1971,1978, Schmidt, et. al., 1989). Male head ornamentation includes a prominent dorsolateral ridge extending on each side from the occipital region forward over the eye, along the dorsolateral border of the snout to the tip or slightly beyond as a small shovel-like projection. The ridge is less prominent in females. Males from some populations (particularly those from the northeastern part of the range) possess a more rounded (as opposed to angular) ridge in the occipital region. There is a low-profiled but well-defined parietal crest on the mid-dorsal line of the caudal half of the head.

The geographic variation of male color has been described in general terms (Bourgat 1970, Brygoo 1971, 1978, Schmidt et al., 1989) and is currently being studied quantitatively by the authors of this section. Adult males from the northwestern insular population (Nosy Bé) tend to be uniformly turquoise or blue-green with spots or patches of red or yellow concentrated on the head and anterior quarter of the torso. The lips are sometimes bright yellow. The degree of facial color is highly variable among individuals and increases with age. While dark vertical bars often appear on the lateral surface of the body and tail when the animal is under stress, these bars are typically faint or absent.

Males from populations along the coast of Madagascar, from the northwestern town of Ambanja ranging eastward around the northern tip of the island and southward along the northeastern coast to at least the town of Sambava, differ subtly from population to population but share a similar basic color pattern during the breeding season. They possess a green body with bold vertical bars of red or blue, or some combination of red and blue. The head, anterior torso, and sometimes the legs and tail are commonly brightly colored with red, orange, or yellow. The degree and patterning of this bright coloration is highly variable among individuals and intensifies dramatically during the peak of the breeding season.

Adult males from populations south of Sambava, along the shores of the Bay of Antongil south to Tamatave, are dark-green to almost black with faint or no vertical bars, a prominent light-colored lateral stripe (males from all populations possess a light or metachromatically variable lateral stripe), and sometimes a distinctly lighter dorsal crest. When displaying to a social partner, males from some of these populations rapidly attain a complete suffusion of red or orange over their entire head, body, legs, and tail. Sometimes distinct dark-green vertical bars are visible on the flanks, legs, and tail. The skin color of the eye turret of all populations is highly metachromatic, changing from a solid color in nondisplay contexts to a pattern of bars radiating from the pupil in social contexts. The color and contrast of these bars is highly variable, both among individuals and among populations.

Adult females from all populations are highly metachromatic, especially when gravid. The basic color of a mature female in a nonsocial context is uniform gray, brown, or faint green with a nondistinct lateral stripe and nondistinct vertical bars. When females are receptive to male courtship, their overall color becomes unpatterned and very pale, or sometimes rich orange to pink. When nonreceptive to courtship they attain a bold pattern of overall dark-brown to black with contrasting vertical bars of pink to orange. A bold lateral stripe of the same color is sometimes present. The borders of these bars are very irregular and highly individualized.

The color of juveniles of both sexes is similar among populations. Immatures are uniformly gray or brown with bold darker vertical bars on the flanks. Some become orange or pink at an early stage and when aroused closely resemble a gravid female in color. More typically, aroused, or cool juveniles, especially young hatchlings, become solid dark-brown, gray or black.

To summarize the geographic distribution, the species occurs along the coast and on the coastal islands of northern and eastern Madagascar from Majunga in the northwest to Tamatave on the east central coast. A record for extreme southern Madagascar (Brygoo 1971) is questionable (Raxworthy, pers. comm.). A small but viable population, supposedly introduced within historic times, occurs on the remote island of Reunion (500 kilometers or 310 miles east of Madagascar). While males from Reunion resemble those from Nosy Bé with overall turquoise coloration, their color pattern is unique in some respects (R. Tremper, S. McKeown, pers. comm.). The species ranges from sea level to about 4,000 feet (or 1,219 m) elevation.

The panther chameleon thrives in a warm, humid climate with little seasonal fluctuation in temperature but with little to fairly dramatic seasonal fluctuation in rainfall. It shuns deeply shaded forest habitat and thrives in forest edge to highly disturbed agricultural and suburban areas. While occasionally climbing to moderate heights (20 feet or 6 meters or so), it is very abundant in small shrubs, bushes, and weeds less than 6 feet (1.8 m) in height. In well-developed forest it may inhabit the crowns of trees (Raxworthy 1988). The grasping power of the feet of the panther chameleon is considerably less than that of the related, slightly larger Oustalet's chameleon with which it is sympatric in the northern part of its range and which can more often be found on thicker, elevated perches.

Despite the high abundance of panther chameleons in some areas, breeding males, juveniles, and nonbreeding females are usually well spaced in the habitat. During the breeding season, males and females commonly coexist in close proximity as a pair, but in late summer and fall adult males and females are more often spatially isolated. Introduction of one individual within clear view of another elicits an immediate behavioral response from a resident. Males are fiercely territorial during the breeding season and will inflict severe damage, or death, if allowed to fight. In the late fall season most adult males are severely scarred, and some are in seriously debilitated condition from fighting.

Panther chameleons seem to prefer warm body temperatures (85 to 95° F or 29.4 to 35° C) and will bask to attain these on cool mornings or days. On warm days they spend most of the daylight hours perched in shade or filtered sun, and their body temperature matches ambient shade temperature very closely within the above range. Unlike some heliophilic lizards they are active on cooler days and in captivity seem to adapt well to ambient temperatures in the mid-80° F (28.9 to 30.6° C).

Panther chameleons prefer appropriate-size arthropods as food. While some individuals readily accept small vertebrates in captivity (such as pinkies and small lizards), others do not. They definitely prefer a variety of prey species and will always orient to a palatable "new" prey item when given a choice. They are voracious feeders, however, and will consume their "usual" prey item if nothing else is available.

Despite their large size, panther chameleons grow rapidly, mature at a young age, produce several clutches (each with 12 to 50 eggs) per season, and experience a high annual turnover in nature. Hatching occurs throughout the warm season (September through April) after a 6-to-12 month incubation. Surviving juveniles are sexually mature by the following warm season. Annual survivorship of mature adults in the field is unknown, but judging by the condition of average- to large-size adult males in May (late fall), it is unlikely that they survive to a second season. Also, considering the high mortality associated with oviposition in captivity, annual turnover for females must be very high. Under optimum indoor growing conditions in captivity hatchlings can reach sexual maturity in less than 6 months (Ferguson 1994).

The length of the breeding season probably varies geographically. In captivity Nosy Bé females cycle continuously and produce a clutch of eggs every 6 to 8 weeks. Nosy Be males appear sexually receptive most of the time, but some have a sexually quiescent period of one to three months. In the field in May (late fall), juveniles of all sizes were present and more than 50 percent of the adult females were gravid. These factors suggest a prolonged breeding season. In all other populations the breeding season appears to be shorter and better defined. In May small juveniles were not present and only a small percent of females were gravid in Ambanja, Diego Suarez, and Moroansetra. Males from Ambanja and Diego Suarez have short periods of sexual activity in captivity. A short breeding season has been well documented for panther chameleons on Reunion Island (Bourgat 1970). This is the most southern locality for the species and occurs at the edge of the true southern tropical zone.

Conservation Status

The panther chameleon, like all Old World chameleons, is listed as Appendix II by CITES (Convention on International Trade in Endangered Species). Because of their large size, attractiveness, hardiness, and accessibility, they have become prime targets for exportation by the commercial trade since Madagascar relaxed its restrictions on exporting lizards in 1987. Exportation increased steadily from 1986 to 1990, when more than 2,000 were legally exported (Anonymous, 1993). They are regularly advertised on lists of most of the wholesale dealers in the United States.

Without some regulation, commercial exploitation could threaten some populations on a local level. Considering their inability to secrete themselves into inaccessible shelters (holes and crevices) and their preference for low perches, it is possible that an entire local population can be removed in a short time from a specified area with intensive daytime and nighttime collecting over a few days. A complete removal in early spring before the first oviposition, followed by a complete removal in late fall when most of the previous years's eggs have hatched, could seriously affect—if not eliminate—that local population. On the other hand, if collecting is *confined* to a restricted area or series of small areas within a large, well-dispersed population, these areas would probably be completely restocked by immigration within a year. By staggering the exploitation of several such areas, a long-term sustained yield could be maintained indefinitely without harming the population. Such a strategy has been employed by commercial collectors of the green anole *Anolis carolinensis* in the southeastern United States.

While this species is basically "weedy" and unlikely to be threatened by forest destruction or moderate collection pressure, some regulation of collection and exportation seems warranted. Restriction of collecting to the mid-to-late breeding season (say, mid-January to mid-February) would allow adults to produce at least one clutch and still be in reasonably robust condition. While the life expectancy of adults at that time would be only a few months in the field, well-maintained captives treated for parasites and maintained free of social strife will survive considerably longer (two to five years). Moderate to large juveniles at that time should undergo considerable density-dependent mortality as they establish home ranges for the next breeding season. So reducing the density of this age class will increase the survival probability of those remaining or hatching late. Many of those removed, instead of dying, will make robust captives with a high probability of breeding and long-term survival.

Probably the most potentially significant impact of this species for chameleon conservation is three-fold. First, it is sufficiently appealing and hardy to make it an ideal candidate for large-scale managed breeding, both in "chameleon farms" in Madagascar and in first-world consumer countries. Such endeavors, which are beginning, would be profitable to commercial herpetologists and would satiate much of the consumer market for captive chameleons in the zoo, educational research, and private sectors. This, with legislative "guidance," could remove much of the exploitation pressure on the more fragile, threatened species. Second, the panther chameleon can serve as a model species to develop and standardize nutrition and husbandry techniques for chameleons in general. While other more threatened species with different ecological niches are likely to vary in their husbandry requirements, sound knowledge of one or a few species will serve as a good starting

Male panther chameleon in the field at Nosy Bé. Photo by Gary Ferguson.

Hatchling panther chameleon. Photo by Gary Ferguson.

point to develop techniques for establishing satellite colonies of species with restricted distributions, or from fast-disappearing habitat, before they are critically endangered. Projects to study the husbandry of the panther chameleon and other common species are underway.

Third and perhaps most important, mainstream conservationists probably have seriously underestimated the inevitability of future degradation of many tropical ecosystems. Even if slash-and-burn agriculture, land development, and human-population growth come to a screeching halt in Madagascar, global warming caused by first-world technology may be great enough to cause changes in climate that result in significant warming and drying of much of Madagascar's original rain forest (Houghton and Woodwell, 1989; Schneider, 1989). Forty of Madagascar's 53 chameleon species (the rainforest endemics) may become "naturally" extinct with this climatic change. Madagascar's chameleon fauna may have to adaptively radiate all over again. In this scenario, hardy generalized species, which are genetically diverse geographically and which can serve as founders for adaptive radiation, take on special importance. Panther chameleons, along with other "weedy" species like *C. oustaleti* and *C. lateralis,* are excellent candidates. Steps should be taken to preserve their diversity, especially in the wild but also in captivity. The long-term persistence of even these weedy species cannot be taken for granted, as the current decline of common frog species indicates (Bishop and Pettit, 1992).

Male panther chameleons are among one of the more "personable" of the true chameleons. Photo by Bill Love.

Panther Chameleon *(Chamaeleo pardalis)*

Captive Management

Since 1988 the panther chameleon has become readily available in the commercial trade. As of June 1992 twelve U.S. zoos reported 17 males, 10 females, 10 juveniles. Information compiled by International Species Inventory System (ISIS). In a recent issue (August 1992) of the Chameleon Information Network, 45 individuals, including many non-professionals, report experience with this species. The breeding potential of a pair of panther chameleons is enormous. Under ideal conditions one can expect from 30 to 150 viable eggs in a year, depending on the number and size of clutches produced. The incubation plus growth period of the eggs and hatchlings can range from 10 to 18 months. So in two and a half years from initial purchase of a pair, one could conceivably be incubating from 450 to 11,250 viable second-generation eggs!

The value of the current captive population as a conservation-oriented satellite population is severely limited, however, for several reasons. The major problem is that the locality of origin of imported specimens is unknown, especially for females. While subspecies are currently not recognized formally, the species varies greatly geographically in morphology, physiology, behavior, and ecology. Many of the captive-produced hatchlings will be interpopulational hybrids that might be poorly adapted to any current natural habitat in Madagascar. Only a few exporters seem interested in providing locality data, which would vastly increase the value of the specimens for scientific or conservation projects. Although the current need for a satellite population to help preserve the species seems small, exporters and importers should realize the importance of providing locality data. Keepers should also realize the importance of keeping good bloodline records for captive-produced hatchlings.

Another problem with captive management of panther chameleons is variable reproductive success past the first captive generation. While first-generation captive hatchlings maintained exclusively indoors grow, survive, and reproduce well in captivity, there are often problems with egg hatchability of these reproductive efforts (Ferguson, 1994). The problem is likely nutritional in origin, relating to dietary vitamins A and D and to calcium (Annis, 1992; Ferguson and Talent, unpublished data; *see below*).

Total or partial outdoor maintenance is desirable when feasible. Ultraviolet-B rays from sunlight generate and help regulate vitamin D synthesis (Holick 1985). Because fat-soluble vitamins may interact in the body (Frig and Broz, 1984; Annis, 1992), the sun may help to inhibit the pathological effects of dietary overdose of other fat-soluble vitamins such as A, E, K, or B. This effect of sunlight remains undocumented for any animal, but most keepers believe that animals raised outdoors have fewer developmental and reproductive problems caused by nutrition. Conversely, unpredictable weather changes, predators, escape, and security add risks to outdoor maintenance. Satisfactory artificial sources of UV-B are available for indoor maintenance.

Captive management of this species should begin while the species is available for exportation. An organized effort should arrange for importation of cohorts from at least six populations *accompanied by locality data*. A studbook should be established, and specimens should be made available to zoos and qualified nonprofessional chameleon keepers who are willing to participate in the studbook project. (Contracts should be signed.) The inevitable surplus should be made available to the open market with proceeds returned to support the continuation of the established genetic lines.

Husbandry Parameters

Housing

In captivity panther chameleons seem to adapt to a wide variety of enclosure designs. Enclosures ranging from several meters on a side to those as small as 12 inches by 12 inches by 18 inches (30.5 cm by 30.5 cm by 45.1 cm) for adult males have proven satisfactory. Small enclosures should be opaque on at least three sides and are recommended only if large numbers must be kept in a small area. In small all-transparent terraria the chameleons may sit on the floor and "paw" at the sides for extended periods. Because panther chameleons (especially some individuals from Nosy Bé) are more active than the average chameleon, they may not be the best species to keep free-ranging in a tree in a garden room or an enclosed porch. They may frequently drop to the floor or wander into areas where they can cause mischief or injure themselves. Unlike some chameleons, they do not seem to require vegetation for security. In any case, most specimens don't show tendencies to hide in vegetation or to show camouflaging behaviors when approached. Most specimens adapt readily to gentle handling.

In designing a customized enclosure, a mesh floor with a tray located underneath is recommended. This is a standard design for bird and small-mammal enclosures. Feces and dripping water that may overflow from a watering dish resting on the mesh floor will fall to the tray for easy cleaning. Feces will be out of contact range for a chameleon walking on the floor of a cage. It is *critical* that any mesh used for chameleon cages be plastic coated or otherwise smooth in texture. Several keepers have reported serious foot or snout damage to chameleons kept in enclosures constructed with standard half-inch hardware cloth or similar rough-textured wire mesh. Even in smooth-mesh enclosures, nose-rubbing may occur if the chameleon perceives desirable environmental factors outside the cage (as in the case of a male seeing a female ready to breed). Individuals in mesh cages should be watched closely to prevent this.

Gravid female panther chameleon in an indoor enclosure with a nesting box containing potting soil.
Photo by Gary Ferguson.

16   Panther Chameleon *(Chamaeleo pardalis)*

Outdoor enclosures for keeping panther chameleons. Photo by Gary Ferguson.

Ideal indoor-outdoor enclosures for panther chameleons are standard wire birdcages with plastic bottoms. Ideal mesh size for moderate to large panther chameleons is 1 inch by $^1/_2$ inch (2.5 cm by 1.3 cm) or long wires spaced $^1/_2$ inch (1.3 cm) apart. Insects can pass through mesh of this size and must be contained in such an enclosure. It is essential that enclosures be well ventilated and not include glass or transparent plastic on sides that are exposed to direct sunlight; otherwise, lethally high temperatures may result.

Environmental Concerns

Panther chameleons tolerate a wide variety of environments. The most inflexible consideration for their well-being is moderately high environmental temperature. While they can tolerate ranges from less than 48° F (8.9° C) to more than 100° F (37.8° C), such extremes are not recommended. Room, cage, or outdoor temperature should vary from 65° F (18.3° C) at night to 90° F (32.2° C) during the day. If maximum environmental temperatures are below 85° F (29.4° C), a daytime hot spot should be available for basking. If an incandescent light bulb of higher than 25 watts is used, it should be protected to prevent the animal from contact burns.

Panther chameleons tolerate diverse light intensity and quality. For aesthetic reasons the more light the better. Skylights and insolation of the cage from a window or fluorescent lighting show off the bright colors of the animal better and may actually cause physiological or behavioral enhancement of its color. For proper nutrition and successful breeding, ultraviolet-B light seems critical. Indoors, one hour per day of fluorescent sunlamp (fs-40 or equivalent) will provide adequate UV-B under the following conditions: (1) at least 30 cm (11.8 in.) from the animal, (2) outside rather than inside cage mesh-work, (3) a gradient is provided inside the cage so that the animal can perch comfortably in full shade from the bulb. Careless use of FS-40 bulbs can be dangerous to the keeper. Lower intensity UV-B provided by blacklights or Vita-Lites® are not adequate for this purpose. Preliminary indications are that illumination from a double Reptisun® or Reptiiguana Light® UVB-310 (available from Zoo Med, San Luis Obispo, CA) for 12 hours per day at distances closer than 30 cm (11.8 in.) should substitute for a sunlamp and would be less likely to cause UV-B or UV-C damage. Further evaluation is necessary to solidify this claim.

Despite the high humidity (daytime humidities sometimes exceed 70 percent on clear summer days) of their habitat, panther chameleons do not seem to require this in captivity. Some report that cage humidities below 35 percent cause shedding problems (R. Tremper, pers. comm.). We have observed no shedding problems at air humidities of 40 to 50 percent. Regardless of the humidity of the air, it is very important to keep the cage interior, especially perches, completely dry, to prevent infections. A drinking system with water dripping into a small overflow dish that in turn drips through a mesh cage floor will be readily used by the panther chameleon, and most individuals will eventually drink from the dish without water dripping. Suitable drippers include: medical IV drippers, suspended ice cubes, and suspended rodent drinking bottles heated with a light bulb. Some keepers prefer to handwater individuals daily with a pipette or spray bottle, but this is labor-intensive if one must manage a large collection. Juveniles kept indoors in small glass or plastic terraria will readily drink drops from the sides after a light misting.

Panther chameleons experience variable seasonal climatic fluctuations in the wild. The typical seasons in Madagascar include warmer, wet summers and cooler, dry winters. Within the panther chameleon's range summer temperatures (day and night averaged) are around 80° F (26.6° C). Winter temperatures are around 72° F (22.2° C). These averages differ little throughout the range of the species, including Reunion

Island. Seasonal rainfall fluctuations vary more across the range of the species. The least seasonal fluctuation in rainfall occurs on Nosy Bé and along the east coast south of Sambava. The greatest seasonal fluctuation is in the north and northwestern parts of Madagascar where the natural ecosystem is savannah (grassland with scattered trees and woodlots) and on Reunion.

So far, first-generation captive panther chameleons seem to breed readily, and those from the more seasonal areas seem to cycle spontaneously without artificial temperature and moisture cycling. More information on second- and later-generational captives may reveal some need for this in panther chameleons from some localities.

Social Management

The best way to maintain panther chameleons is one animal per small-to-moderate-size enclosure. Juveniles can be maintained in small groups *if* food is available *ad libitum* and if there is opportunity for visual isolation provided by vegetation or partial partitioning. The same may hold true for adults as long as there is only one adult male per group and the most aggressive females are removed. (See further discussion under *propagation techniques.*) If hatchlings are initially crowded in small terraria (10 per one-cubic-foot or 30.5-cubic-cm enclosure) without the opportunity for visual isolation, they will tolerate such crowding fairly well for several weeks, as long as adequate food is available. However, if hatchlings are isolated for even a very short period (one week) and allowed to feed and thermoregulate, their tolerance to subsequent crowding is greatly reduced. Adult males are so territorially aggressive that they will severely injure or kill each other if kept together when in breeding condition.

Nutritional Requirements

While there is considerable knowledge about some elements of nutrition in this and other chameleon species, our greatest ignorance also lies in this area. Many failures of captive management of chameleons by serious herpetoculturists probably result from our ignorance about proper nutritional balance.

In a recent laboratory study, food intake of panther chameleons under *ad libitum* conditions was quantified from hatching to maturity (Ferguson, 1991; Ferguson, 1994). Growing chameleons consume a mass of appropriate-size insects up to an equivalent of their body mass per week. Individuals fed at levels not promoting rapid growth languish and die. Full-size adults of either sex will maintain their body mass and reproduce when eating about 30 to 50 adult crickets per week (about 7 to 12 grams or 0.25 to 0.4 oz).

There are several considerations when presenting food to chameleons. The large numbers of active insects that panther chameleons require should be contained in such a way that they are readily available to the animal without in turn causing it irritation or harm. For example, if 10 to 20 crickets are offered to a chameleon in a small plastic terrarium, say of 3 to 5 gallons (11.4 to 19 liters) in volume, the terrarium should contain high perches not touching the floor and a small refuge on the floor for the crickets. The chameleon can retreat to the perch and avoid having crickets crawl over it. In large enclosures, and in those with mesh walls whose mesh spacing is large enough for crickets or other active insects to escape, the insects should be confined in opaque cups at least 6 inches (15.2 cm) deep. The sides of the cups should be opaque, so that the chameleons will not attempt to feed through the walls, and slick, so that the insects will not climb out. A curtain pin or similar device attached to the outside rim will allow the cup to be hung below a favorite perch so that the insects can be seen by the chameleon. If *ad libitum* availability is desired, food and water *must* be continually available to the insects. Hungry crickets not only become nutritionally depleted within a 24-hour period but, unless well contained, they will actively seek out and attack the soft tissue of the chameleon while it is sleeping and defenseless.

As we have previously mentioned, a serious gap in our knowledge concerns nutritional quality requirements. Although most herpetoculturists believe that crickets, mealworms, and waxworms do not provide a balanced diet for most lizards, opinions vary widely about how much of which nutrient supplements are needed. A major difficulty is that some nutrients—particularly calcium, vitamin A, and vitamin D—are toxic if given in too large a dose. Another serious problem is that nutrient requirements and tolerances may differ between species or even between closely related populations of the same species (L. Talent, pers. comm.). Juveniles, adult males, and adult females, or even individuals within one of these groups may differ. Well-controlled experiments with carefully manipulated and administered doses and large sample sizes are necessary to increase our understanding of these critical issues. Keeping animals outdoors, where they can receive natural levels of ultraviolet-B radiation, and feeding them a large variety of *wild* insect species is currently the only way to guarantee freedom from nutritional problems. Some keepers have reported cases of gout resulting from a diet that includes too many pinkie mice or wax-worms (S. McKeown, pers. comm.).

Vitamin and mineral supplements can be provided as powder directly applied to insects by agitating or "dusting" them in a plastic bag or cup. Such powders also can cover the bottom of feeding containers and will be secondarily picked up by the chameleon's tongue when it feeds. An effective and preferred alternative involves feeding the supplement to the insect, or "gut-loading." The level of supplementation can be more effectively controlled and monitored by this method, suffocating the insect with the dust can be avoided, as can the insect's active attempt to remove the dusted supplement. Crickets, which are voracious omnivores, are excellent subjects for gut-loading (Allen and Oftedal, 1989).

Juveniles and reproducing females seem to require higher doses of calcium and vitamin D_3 than adult males; however, fortification of cricket food with 8 percent calcium by weight, especially in combination with high dietary vitamin D, can cause soft-tissue mineralization. This can ultimately prove fatal; thus, lower calcium concentrations in cricket food are recommended. Preliminary results of current experiments strongly suggest that endogenous vitamin D produced by exposure to ultraviolet-B irradiation is necessary for continued health and successful reproduction of panther chameleons. While high levels of dietary vitamin D_3 can maintain or restore hatching success (for adult females, 100 IU or International Units per month by mouth, divided into weekly doses; L. Talent, pers. comm.), it can also cause toxemia and can shorten the life of a female.

Growing juveniles seem to require cricket-food fortification levels of 50 to 100 IU of vitamin A per gram of cricket food to prevent symptoms such as loss of muscular coordination, spinal and tail kinking or abnormal flexure, eye closure, skin lesions, or hemipenal impactions (in males). This dose for adult females seems to be the minimum necessary for production of healthy eggs and may be close to deficient. Levels that cause vitamin A overdose symptoms have not yet been determined, but for females direct administration by mouth of 150 IU per month (divided into weekly doses) appears to result in healthy hatchlings (L. Talent, pers. comm.). Vitamin A overdose symptoms include gular fluid retention (edema), kidney failure, sterility, metabolic bone disease (caused by bone decalcification), or failure to ovulate in adult females. Vitamin A requirements for panther chameleons may be totally inappropriate for other chameleon species (Annis 1992).

In nature vitamin A is probably manufactured by the animals themselves from vitamin precursors such as beta-carotene rather than ingested directly in their diet. Thus, gut-loading crickets with carotenoid-rich vegetables such as carrots, squash, turnip greens, or mustard greens may be a safer method of vitamin A supplementation.

Health

The greatest cause of premature mortality in panther chameleons that are given proper care, as outlined above, seems to be parasitic infestation and disease brought in from the wild. A critically important consideration when obtaining recent imports is season. In the Malagasy spring and summer (October through March) adults are actively breeding, undergoing serious territorial disputes, and accumulating high parasite loads. In early spring robust adults and small juveniles may be obtained. In late spring adults are still in robust condition, but some treatment for parasites may be necessary if fecal exams reveal their presence. After December the condition of adults deteriorates until May, when most adults are probably too debilitated to survive long in captivity, even if they survive the rigors of exportation. *Only* mid-size to large juveniles or small adult wild-caught specimens should be obtained after early March.

Healthy adult males obtained in the Malagasy springtime can be expected to survive from two to five years in captivity. Females should survive from one to two years. Improved knowledge of nutritional requirements might extend captive life expectancies in the future.

Reproduction

Sexing Techniques

While sexing mature adult panther chameleons is easy, sexing immatures can be tricky. Immature males, especially hatchlings, usually (but not always) have a slightly thicker tail base than do females; however, hatchling males have a vestigial pair of hemipenal pockets that almost invariably give the underside of the tail-base a more gently tapered profile toward the cloacal aperture. Females sometimes have more orange or pink on the body and more red or orange on the interstitial skin of the gular region, but this is not absolute and can vary geographically. Using these criteria, especially tail-base taper, one can with a little practice sex hatchlings with greater than 90 percent accuracy.

Propagation Techniques

To breed panther chameleons several set ups seem appropriate. Adults can be maintained in isolation and one individual can be periodically introduced into the enclosure of a different-sex individual. If individuals are hand-tamed, merely opening the cage door of an individual and holding the other, perched on one's hand, in view will elicit a social response and dictate the next step. It doesn't matter which sex is the resident unless the individuals differ in temperament. Then the tamer individual should be the nonresident. Sometimes an isolated male will court too aggressively when first viewing a female. This may elicit a nonreceptive response in a physiologically receptive female. In this case the two should be put into visual contact but with actual contact prevented. For example, if a male is in a large display cage, a female can be put into a small plastic terrarium, which in turn is placed into the larger enclosure. Usually after a few minutes to a couple of hours, the male will habituate to the female's presence and approach her with more ritualized courtship. Females become receptive to courtship spontaneously upon reaching mature size and within two to three weeks after oviposition. This receptivity is readily apparent by the light-

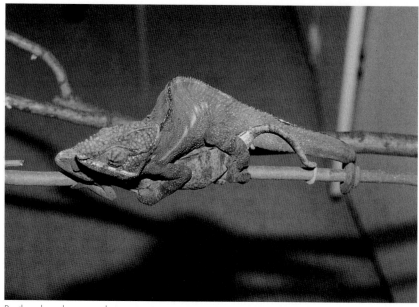

Panther chameleons copulating. Photo by Gary Ferguson.

ening or brightening of her color and by the subduction of any patterned markings. This display occurs in the absence of her viewing a male. If it persists after she first sees a male, she is ready to mate. The pair can be left together for several days to a couple of weeks, until the female displays nonreceptive color (bold patterning) and behavior (side-to-side rocking with open mouth and lateral compression).

Virgin females will remain in a state of receptivity for up to three months. If the period of waiting has been very long, she will probably assume nonreceptivity immediately or within a few minutes after the first copulation. If placed with a male shortly after becoming sexually receptive (within a few days), she may allow several copulations over a period of several days or a couple of weeks. Nonvirgin females spontaneously assume nonreceptivity after a few days if not given an opportunity to breed. Usually, eggs fertilized from stored sperm are deposited three to six weeks later. With this protocol bred females should be returned to isolation. After three to six weeks females will become increasingly restless and eggs will become detectable by gentle palpation. At this time nesting substrate from 6 to 12 inches (15.2 to 30.5 cm) deep should be added to the enclosure. (It can be contained in a rectan-

At left a two month old female panther chameleon and at right a three month old female panther chameleon. Photo by Gary Ferguson.

gular or cylindrical container placed within her enclosure if space permits.) Alternatively, the female can be removed and placed in an opaque one-to-five-gallon (3.8-to-19-liter) container filled halfway with moist (*not* wet) sand, potting soil, or a combination of the two. Remove her after two days if she does not begin nest excavation, and reintroduce her in two days. Do not allow insects to roam free in the container as they may bother her or attack the eggs. Several keepers have reported a preference by females to dig and nest into the root systems of potted plants (S. McKeown, 1991; C. DeWitt, pers. comm.). This makes good ecological sense because the open soil in many areas where the species exists becomes extremely dry and brick-hard. In such areas, a plant's root systems may be the only place where nests can be constructed and eggs can remain hydrated. Gravid females not given an opportunity to dig a nest will usually oviposit on the floor of the cage, where the eggs will quickly dehydrate and die. Sometimes under these conditions they will retain one to several eggs, which can lead to uterine infections and death; therefore, it is important to keep track of breeding dates and not delay in providing an egg-laying site.

Alternative to isolation of the male and female with periodic short-term cohabitation, permanent pairs or breeding groups ranging up to 1 male and 5 females can be maintained. With this method the cage should be a minimum of 6 feet (1.8 m) high by 4 feet (1.2 m) long by 4 feet (1.2 m) deep (the larger the better), large enough for individuals to space themselves. Success with groups including multiple females has been mixed. The group should be watched carefully and "trouble maker" (aggressively dominant) females removed immediately. Individuals raised together since hatching may more likely be compatible. Food and water should be available *ad libitum*. The onset of nonreceptivity of each female should be noted; females may have to be paint-marked for easy recognition by the keeper. Nonreceptive females should be carefully watched for nesting if permanent nesting substrate is available or, if it is not available, restless females should be removed as described above. Whether or not life expectancy is different in such permanent breeding groups has not been verified, but, as noted above, breeding males and females are in pairs and seem well spaced in the field when not actively breeding (see also Bourgat, 1970). As previously noted, panther chameleons from some populations have well-defined short breeding seasons, while those from other populations breed most of the year. The timing of receptivity and the duration of gestation varies among females but is fairly predictable among cycles of the same female.

Incubation Techniques

The standard technique for incubating chameleon eggs involves spacing the eggs in a vermiculite-filled container that is sealed or semi-sealed to contain moisture. This technique works well for panther chameleons although it is unnatural. In the field, chameleons construct burrows and lay eggs in a compact mass. The presence of an egg chamber containing an air pocket has not been verified. Indeed, when excavating eggs from a nest box one gains the impression that such a chamber is absent. Some herpetoculturists have experienced persistent death of chameleon eggs at term (just prior to hatching) with this and other species. Although this is probably a maternal effect related to nutrition or excessive moisture in most cases, the possible need for socially induced hatching cues (such as tactile cues or the moisture of hatching neighbors) has not been ruled out for chameleons.

Vermiculite moisture during incubation should average around -400 KiloPascals (about 0.7 parts water to 1.0 part dry vermiculite by weight for average grained vermiculite). Too much moisture can cause egg bursting and death caused by suffocation of the neonate at term.

Panther chameleon eggs in incubator. Photo by Gary Ferguson.

Incubation Temperature and Diapause

Panther chameleon eggs seem to tolerate a fairly wide range of incubation temperatures. These temperatures influence the duration of incubation, which has been reported to range from 180 to 365 days (Bourgat, 1970; Schmidt, et al., 1989). Many chameleon species, including the panther chameleon, lay eggs at a very early stage of development. The egg remains at this stage for a defined period of time; that is, it remains in diapause before initiating further development (Blanc, 1974). In captivity panther chameleon eggs maintained at a water potential averaging -400 Kpa, and at a day-to-night fluctuating environmental temperature ranging from 65 to 78° F (18.3 to 25.5° C), hatch in 7 to 10 months. The variation seems to be caused by a variable diapause period of 3 to 6 months.

The post-diapause initiation of development can be recognized by candling the eggs with strong backlighting. A shift from yellow to pink transmitted light indicates development of blood islets, and that dynamic development is in progress. In some Malagasy chameleons diapause can be prolonged for up to a year if kept at improper temperatures (too high). Infertile or dead eggs spoil rapidly (one week after oviposition or death). Therefore, never discard healthy eggs, no matter how long they have been incubating.

Excavated nest of panther chameleon. Photo by Gary Ferguson.

The duration of diapause in the panther chameleon can be influenced by high and low temperatures. A constant incubation temperature of 82° F (27.8° C) prolongs diapause by two months (Ferguson, 1994). A constant incubation temperature of 65° F (18.3° C) for one or two months followed by a return to the fluctuating temperature range previously cited will break diapause before three months (Ferguson, unpublished data). Because panther chameleon eggs overwinter in Madagascar, cooler winter temperatures may prime eggs still in diapause to initiate development upon the return of warmer springtime temperatures. This might synchronize the hatching of eggs laid at different times, especially if high late summer and fall temperatures prolong diapause.

Eggs are very robust to handling, especially when in diapause. After that they may be handled but orientation of the egg should not be changed. Newly laid eggs or eggs still in diapause (showing yellow transmitted light) can be shipped without damage as long as extreme temperatures are avoided.

A method for raising individual panther chameleon babies using glass goldfish bowls.
Photo by Gary Ferguson.

Egg Hatching and Neonates

Healthy neonates generally do not require special treatment at hatching. At term, egg permeability increases, beads of moisture form on the egg surface, and egg dimension decreases noticeably. The neonate slits the egg shell within a few days of these events and usually remains within the egg shell for one or two days, while resorbing the external yolk sac. If the shell is not slit by the neonate at this time, the neonate dies. Some herpetologists recommend vigorous spraying of the egg with water or saline solution after the first signs of shell permeability appear. Although this may not be essential for healthy neonates, one should take care to avoid placing the egg in a dry environment between the period of slitting and emergence. To do so may cause shell drying and entrapment of the neonate. If the first few neonates fail to slit the shell and die, one can expect problems with the entire clutch. Vigorous spraying may aid emergence of the few strongest individuals. Alternatively, manual slitting of the egg may have the same result.

Neonates will readily adapt to simple small indoor enclosures such as plastic pet habitats, gallon (3.8 liter) jars or 2-gallon (7.6-liter) aquaria or similar-size outdoor screened enclosures. These should be free of

A hatchling panther chameleon. Photo by Bill Love.

substrate, contain ample climbing perches, and include small hiding places for crickets. A petri dish containing appropriate cricket food should be provided. Crickets one to three millimeters long should be continuously available. If grain diets are fed to the crickets, the cricket food should be fortified with calcium (one to four percent) and with a vitamin mixture containing vitamins A and D (50 to 100 IU of each vitamin per gram of cricket food). Alternatively, the carotenoid- and calcium-rich vegetable diet for crickets in combination with UV-B irradiation recommended for adults is also recommended for juveniles. With a good cricket diet, "dusting" of crickets is not necessary.

Acknowledgements

Co-authors of this article include: Gary W. Ferguson, Department of Biology, Texas Christian University, Fort Worth, Texas, USA; James B. Murphy, Department of Herpetology, Dallas Zoo,Dallas, Texas, USA; Achille Raselemananana and Jean-Baptiste Ramananmanjato, Department of Biology, University of Antannanarivo, Antannanarivo, Madagascar. The authors wish to thank Bill Gehrmann, Larry Talent, Steve Hammack, Fred Frye, and Michael Holick for interactions critical to the preparation of this chapter.

Literature Cited

Allen, M.E., and O.T. Oftedal. 1989. "Dietary Manipulation of the Calcium Content of Feed Crickets." *J. Zoo and Wildl. Med.* 20: 26–33.

Annis, J. A. 1992. "Hypervitaminosis A in Chameleons: Are We Unknowingly Overdosing Our Animals on Vitamin A?" *Chameleon Information Network* 9: 18–25.

Anonymous. 1993. A Preliminary Review of the Status and Distribution of Reptile and Amphibian Species Exported from Madagascar." Joint Nature Conservation Committee, IUCN/SSC Trade Specialist Group and BIODEV. Cambridge, UK.

Bishop, C.A., and K.E. Pettit, 1992. "Declines in Canadian Amphibian Populations: Designing a National Monitoring Strategy." Occas. Papers Canadian Wildlife Services. 76: 1–120.

Blanc, F. 1974. Table de Dévelopement de *Chamaeleo lateralis* Gray 1831." Ann. dEmbryol. Morphogen. 7: 99–115.

Bourgat, R. 1970. "Recherches Écologiques et Biologiques sur le *Chamaeleo pardalis* Cuvier 1829 de l'Isle de la Réunion et de Madagascar." Bull. Soc. Zool. France 95:259–268.

Brygoo, E.R. 1971. Reptiliens Sauriens Chamaeleonidae. Genre *Chamaeleo*. Faune de Madagascar 33: 1–138.

Brygoo, E.R. 1978. Reptiliens Sauriens Chamaeleonidae. Genre *Brookesia* et Complément pour la Genre *Chamaeleo*. Faune de Madagascar 47: 1–173.

Ferguson, G.W. 1991. "Ad-libitum Feeding Rates, Growth and Survival of Captive-hatched Chameleons (*Chamaeleo pardalis*) from Nosy Bé Island, Madagascar." *Herpetological Rev.* 22: 124–125.

Ferguson, G.W. 1994. "Old-World Chameleons in Captivity: Growth, Maturity and Reproduction of Malagasy Panther Chameleons (*Chamaeleo pardalis*)." In *Captive Management and Conservation of Amphibians and Reptiles*, J.B. Murphy, K. Adler, and J.T. Collins (eds.), *Soc. Stu. Amph. Rept.*, Ithaca, NY. *Contributions to Herpetology*, vol. 11.

Frigg, M., and J. Broz. 1984. "Relationships Between Vitamin A and Vitamin E in the Chick." *Internat. J. Vit. Nutr. Res.* 54: 125–134.

Holick, M.F. 1985. "The Photobiology of Vitamin D and its Consequences for Humans." In *The Medical and Biological Effects of Light*, R.J. Wurtman, M.J. Baum, J.T. Potts (eds.). New York Acad. Sci. New York.

Houghton, R.A., and G.M. Woodwell. 1989. "Global Climatic Change." *Scientific American*. 260: 36–44.

McKeown, S. 1991. "Second-Generation Panther Chameleons Bred at the Chaffee Zoo." *Amer. Assoc. Zool. Parks Aquar. Communique*. August: 14.

Raxworthy, C.J. 1988. "Reptiles, Rainforest and Conservation in Madagascar." *Biol. Conserv.* 43: 181–211.

Schmidt, W.K., K. Tamm, E. Wallikewitz. 1989. *Chamäleons: Drachen unserer Zeit.* Herpetologischer Fachverlag, Münster. 112 pp.

Schneider, S.H. 1989. "The Changing Climate." *Scientific American.* 261: 70–79.

Part II

Jackson's Chameleon
(*Chamaeleo jacksonii*)
Natural History, Captive Management, and Breeding

by Sean McKeown

Chameleons, Family Chamaeleonidae

Chameleons are primarily an African and Madagascan group of highly specialized, arboreal, insectivorous lizards comprising more than 130 described species. All the Madagascan forms that have been studied are egg-layers, whereas some of the African forms, including the Jackson's chameleon, give birth to live young (Glaw and Vences, 1994). For much of the twentieth century, chameleons were placed in their own suborder, Rhiptoglossa; however, taxonomists have recently reclassified chameleons. They are now considered to be related to the agamids and iguanids and have been placed into their own subfamily within the Chamaeleonidae (Glaw and Vences, 1994; Zug, 1993).

Jackson's Chameleons, *Chamaeleo jacksonii*

The Jackson's chameleon *(Chamaeleo jacksonii)* was originally described by the Belgium-born curator of the British Museum of Natural History, G.A. Boulenger, in 1896. His initial description was based on a partially grown, preserved male specimen that had been donated to the museum by F.J. Jackson. Strangely, the title of the article describing this initial specimen was "Description of a New Chameleon from Uganda" (Boulenger, 1896). The actual label on the type specimen, however, clearly indicated that it was collected in the vicinity of Nairobi, in the Kikuyu District of Kenya, in what was then part of British East Africa (Eason, Ferguson, and Hebrard, 1988). Several years later, in 1903, Tornier described what he called *C. j. vauerescecae* from Nairobi. Approximately half a century later, in 1959, the Dutch herpetologist Dick Hillenius invalidated this subspecies as he found individuals of *C. j. jacksonii* in the general area of their type locality (Nairobi) that clearly fell within the range of Tornier's description (Hillenuis, 1959). At about the same time, A. Stanley Rand of the Smithsonian Institution described a smaller form, the Mt. Meru Jackson's chameleon, *C. j. merumontana* (Rand, 1958). Finally, 30 years later, Perri Eason, Gary W. Ferguson, and James Hebrard undertook field work in East Africa that led to the formal description of a "new" subspecies, a form already well known to herpetoculturists: the Mt. Kenya yellow-crested Jackson's chameleon, *C. j. xantholophus*. This significant paper also provided an important overview of variation in *Chamaeleo jacksonii* (Eason, Ferguson, and Hebrard, 1988).

The Jackson's chameleon is a mid-size arboreal member of the genus *Chamaeleo*, indigenous to the neighboring countries of Kenya and Tanzania in East Africa. The nominate form, *C. j. jacksonii*, occurs at areas of mid-elevation in the vicinity of Nairobi, north of the western and southwestern slopes of Mount Kenya and the Aberdare Mountains. It is found at an elevation of 5,000 feet (1,520 m) around Nairobi and at up to 8,000 feet (2,440 m) on Mt. Kenya and the Aberdares. So far, the Mt. Meru Jackson's chameleon *(C. j. merumontana)* has been documented only from the Mr. Meru region of Tanzania at mid- and high elevations. The yellow-crested Jackson's chameleon, *C. j. xantholophus* (the subspecies in herpetoculture in the United States), is wide ranging at mid- and high elevations on the east and south slopes of Mt. Kenya (in the country of Kenya) from about 6,000 to 8,000 feet (1,830 to 2,440 m). [Refer to map 1]. On the south slopes of Mt. Kenya are areas of intergradation between *C. j. jacksonii* and *C. j. xantholophus.*

The Eason, Ferguson, and Hebrard study found five statistically independent morphological factors in females and four in male Jackson's chameleons that accounted for the variation between known populations of this species. I have summarized the most important data in Table 1.

Habitat Use in the Wild in East Africa

Jackson's chameleons are most commonly found in Kenya and Tanzania in mid- to high elevations where rainfall averages more than 50 inches (127 cm) per year; however, the areas used by these lizards have both wet and dry seasons. Hence, the degree of humidity and the temperature fluctuation, depending on the time of the year. Daytime temperatures typically range from 60 to 80° F (16 to 27° C), with nighttime temperatures averaging 40 to 65° F (4 to 18° C), depending on the time of year and the specific locality.

With the burgeoning of the human populations in these two African countries during the second half of the twentieth century, large

Table 1: Key to the Three Subspecies of Jackson's Chameleon (*Chamaeleo jacksonii*)

Diagnostic Variables	*C.j. jacksonii*	*C.j. merumontana*	*C.j. xantholophus*
Snout-to-vent size (the length of the head and body, not including the tail	4.13 inches (105 mm)	3.1 inches (78 mm)	4.9 inches (124 mm)
Rostral (snout) horn in females (the horn at the top of the front of the head)	prominent	prominent	either absent or greatly reduced in size
Preocular horns in females (the two horns just above and in front of the eyes)	from absent to fully developed	typically absent	either absent or greatly reduced in size
Parietal crest pigmentation (color of the ridge at the back of the head)	dark or dusky	dusky or light	light, usually yellow in color
Size of scales at top of parietal crest in males	raised and rough appearing	not enlarged and smooth	not enlarged and smooth
Most characteristic features to distinguish each	intermediate size; has a greater number of interorbital scales than *C. j. merumontana*	smaller size and has a lower number of interorbital scales than *C. j. jacksonii*	largest size; yellow crest

areas of forest have been burned or cleared for agriculture. Fortunately, Jackson's chameleons are generalists and very opportunistic. While they are common in the canopy and edge of primary forested areas, they also have adapted very well to secondary forest and disturbed areas. Crops such as coffee, tea, mangoes, and bananas have created increased numbers of insects—including flies, bees, crickets, and grasshoppers—which these lizards readily consume. Population densities of Jackson's chameleons are generally higher in some of the disturbed and agricultural areas than they are in the remaining forests in the national parks (Ferguson, Murphy, and Hudson, 1990).

During the early 1960s, Jackson's chameleons were occasionally available in very small numbers from the few reptile importers in the United States. During the late 1960s and the 1970s, when more and more people became interested in reptiles and amphibians, Jackson's chameleons were exported by the thousands each year from Kenya. The primary exporter was Jonathan Leakey, son of the famous anthropologists Louis and Mary Leakey. Most animals that Jonathan Leakey sent overseas were collected for him by local people off the slopes of

Mt. Kenya. Virtually all the chameleons were the large yellow-crested race, *C. j. xantholophus*. The price that dealers in America paid for them was $3 per lizard. The chameleons were generally retailed in the United States for $35 each. Then, in 1981, the Kenyan government totally shut down the trade in Jackson's chameleons. These lizards were declared a "game species," which meant that each lizard would now cost many hundreds of dollars apiece for a "take" permit to be issued. No more Jackson's chameleons left Kenya for the United States, Great Britain, Western Europe, or Japan.

How Jackson's Chameleons Became Available to the Herpetoculturist

In 1972, a pet shop owner in Kaneohe on the island of Oahu, Hawaii, was issued a permit by the Hawaii State Department of Agriculture to import one dozen Jackson's chameleons. They were obtained from a large southern California reptile wholesaler. The lizards quickly sold, and another permit for several dozen was issued. This second group of Jackson's chameleons arrived thin and dehydrated, having been held indoors by the dealer for several weeks after receipt. Thinking that the chameleons could be retrieved as needed, the pet shop owner released the lizards to recover in his well-planted backyard on Kaneohe Bay Drive in Kaneohe, on the windward side of Oahu (McKeown, 1978).

Chameleons from this initial population spread through the well-planted mesic suburban neighborhood. By the late 1970s, populations of Jackson's were established along nearby watershed areas at the base of the Koolau Mountains (McKeown, 1978). Today, *C. j. xantholophus* occurs in a number of different geographic areas of Oahu. These lizards continue to expand their range. In fact, between 1984 and the present, virtually every wild-caught "Jackson's" (*C. j. xantholophus*) for sale in the continental United States was of Hawaiian origin. Thus, virtually all of the Mt. Kenya Jackson's Chameleons now bred in the United States mainland have Hawaiian forebears (McKeown, 1991).

Jackson's chameleons on Oahu have shown surprising plasticity in adapting both to suburban neighborhoods and to low- and mid-elevation secondary forest, or areas of disturbed vegetation. In addition to natural dispersal, their habit of crossing roadways contributed to their early spread. Upon seeing them walking across a road, motorists often picked them up out of curiosity and later released them in their backyards or at other locations. Many hikers took them home for pets to release in their yard or gave them to neighbors for their yards.

Breeding populations of Mt. Kenya yellow-crested Jackson's chameleons are now well established in a number of areas on Oahu. Although they are most common in the Koolau Range between Kaneohe and Kailua, large breeding populations exist in many disjunct areas throughout Oahu, even at low elevations on the much drier leeward side of the island. Still, these lizards are most abundant at areas of mid-elevation on the windward side of the island. This species is now also well established at mid-elevation at several areas on the Kona side of the Big Island of Hawaii and on the island of Maui. These lizards are most common in secondary forest, in disturbed areas, in various types of orchards, and on hedges in residential yards. In "upcountry Maui" at mid-elevation, at about 2,500 to 3,000 feet (760 to 910 m) around Makawao, they are so plentiful that it is not unusual to see school children selling Jackson's chameleons to passing tourists on weekends. The first reports of Jackson's chameleons on Kauai were in 1995.

During the late 1980s and early 1990s, it was illegal to keep Jackson's chameleons in Hawaii according to the Hawaii State Department of Agriculture, which did not want their distribution to increase in the islands. In 1994, however, after much protest, that ruling was rescinded. As of the time of this writing, Jackson's chameleons are legal to own in Hawaii, and they can be legally bought, sold, and sent to the U.S. mainland. It is still illegal, however, to transfer them between various Hawaiian Islands.

The interest in these lizards in Hawaii has been phenomenal. During weekends, on the main island of Oahu, hundreds of cars are parked along watershed areas while large numbers of people walk through the secondary forest in search of these lizards, which they intend to keep as personal pets or to sell to pet shops. Still other people carry butterfly nets to catch crickets, grasshoppers, large flies, and other insects to feed their pet Jackson's chameleons, because commercially raised insects are unavailable in Hawaii. There is so much disturbed and secondary forest area in Hawaii and such an abundant supply of introduced insects that this relatively low-density species surely will continue to expand its range in the Hawaiian Islands. The author has closely followed the spread of these lizards there and has as yet seen nothing about them that might be regarded as injurious to Hawaii's specialized endemic invertebrate fauna.

In appearance and size, Hawaiian specimens are much like their Mt. Kenya founder stock. The possible exceptions are occasional males with uneven or drooping preocular horns, which may indicate genetic drift. Gary Ferguson has reported to the author, however, that Kenyan specimens sometimes have uneven horns, so variation is seen in African populations as well. Ferguson also believes that horn shape and length may result from a combination of genetics and environment. Under laboratory conditions, high temperatures and improper nutrition produce atypical horn development (Ferguson, pers. com.).

Interestingly, in the Hawaiian Islands Jackson's chameleons are most abundant in areas of moderate rainfall, where daytime temperatures range from the 70 to 90° F (21 to 32° C) and nighttime temperatures vary from 50 to 70° F (10 to 20° C). This temperature range is not too dissimilar from that in their preferred habitats in East Africa, although it is perhaps slightly warmer in some areas.

In addition to the Hawaiian Islands, where large breeding populations occur, tiny populations that appear to be reproductively viable may exist along the coast of California in Morro Bay, Redondo Beach, and San Diego. From time to time, free-ranging individuals turn up at these localities. A Morro Bay population may have originated from a California Department of Fish and Game investigation of a reptile wholesaler living there around 1980. No chameleons were taken, but the agents left open a door to a large outdoor enclosure, and a number of Jackson's chameleons escaped into the surrounding neighborhood.

At irregular intervals, about once a year, a very few of the distinctive Mt. Meru Jackson's chameleons *(C. j. merumontana)* have been legally exported from Tanzania to the United States by expatriate importer Joe Beraducci. These infrequent shipments represent the only *C. jacksonii* still coming out from Africa to the United States commercially.

Lifestyle, Behavior, and Arboreal Adaptations

In the wild, Jackson's chameleons live singly. Each individual has its own territory. Generally, birds are the main predators of chameleons. In East Africa, several nonvenomous and venomous tree snake species also routinely eat chameleons.

Chameleons have been called the masters of camouflage. These lizards rest motionless or move very slowly and deliberately with a rocking gait so they are not seen by potential predators. They have a highly sophisticated ability to vary their skin pigments. Not only do their color-changing abilities help camouflage them, but chameleons are also capable of making their bodies appear more elongate like a twig or branch. By laterally flattening their sides, they can make themselves look like just another leaf on a tree. Their independently rotating eyes, set like turrets, afford unobstructed observation of their surroundings in any direction without having to move their heads or bodies.

The chameleon's ability to change colors has functions other than camouflage. Its normal colors and the intensity of its color signal its moods to other chameleons of the species. As an ectotherm, it can absorb heat from the sun on cool mornings. In the early morning, the chameleon is usually dark so as to absorb infrared heat. Its colors lighten as its body absorbs more heat and its body temperature rises. Chameleons are renowned for the rapid speed of their color change, which occurs through movement of pigment in the skin cells known as chromatophores.

A specialized arboreal feeding adaptation for living in trees is the chameleon's long muscular tongue, which it can rapidly propel to as much as $1\frac{1}{2}$ times its body length to capture insect prey. The tip of the chameleon's tongue is like a moist suction cup that attaches to the prey and rapidly jerks it back into its mouth.

Feet with opposable toes allow the chameleon to grip branches firmly and to move slowly but deliberately between branches in order to feed or to flee. The long tail is also prehensile. At night, it is curled up while the chameleon sleeps. If a portion of its tail is lost, the chameleon cannot regenerate it.

If a snake predator approaches, a Jackson's chameleon can flatten its sides, take on dark colors, open its mouth, hiss, and feign biting by rapidly swinging its head around with its mouth wide open. If a predatory bird threatens a Jackson's chameleon, it can drop from its perching place to the ground and rapidly move to the base of a nearby bush, or it can quickly descend downward into the interior of the bush or tree, where a bird predator cannot follow.

A male chameleon will defend his territory and defend his rights to any nearby female. The horns on a male Jackson's chameleon (and on other chameleon species with preocular and rostral projections) are not merely ornamental. They serve in ritualized combat with other male chameleons of the same species (Bustard, 1958; Rand, 1961).

Virtually all the Jackson's chameleons available in the United States are the larger *C. j. xantholophus* subspecies. An unusually large male can slightly exceed 6 inches (15 cm) in head and body length (not including horns) and have a total length slightly more than 12 inches (30 cm). A more typical adult male specimen is usually about 5 inches (12.7 cm) snout-to-vent length and 10 inches (25.4 cm) in total length. Females usually are slightly more robust but slightly smaller than males.

For Jackson's chameleons, body size is very important in determining whether combat will occur between two males. Typically, a male will spar only with another male of similar size. If one male is dramatically smaller than another, it will retreat out of the larger male's territory. Initially, a male may rub its horn along the branch it is crawling on, as a signal to a relatively nearby male of nearly equal size that it is ready to engage in ritualized combat. The lizards may approach each other from a horizontal or vertical direction, depending on their positions relative to one another on a tree or bush. The two males approach quickly and lock horns. Each male uses its horns to push and shove the other. Typically, these territorial battles last several minutes, with each individual gaining then losing some ground. Finally, the winner is able to force its opponent to lose its foot grip on the branch (during sparring, the tail is not usually employed to grasp) and the loser is forced off, dropping to a lower branch or to the ground. In some contests, one chameleon may be pushed back consistently enough that it chooses to disengage and retreat. With little more than its ego

Map 1. Jackson's chameleons are most commonly found in Kenya and Tanzania in mid–to high elevations where rainfall averages more than 50 inches per year.

deflated, it leaves the immediate area to the winning male. In those situations in which the losing male does not immediately depart, the winning male may pursue, ram, threaten, or attempt to bite until the other lizard moves quickly away.

Selecting a Jackson's Chameleon

Do not purchase a Jackson's chameleon until you have established a proper environment for it. Have ready either a large, portable, screened indoor/outdoor enclosure on rollers. Minimum size should be 2 feet (61 cm) long by 2 feet (61 cm) wide by 3 feet (91 cm) high or both an indoor and an outdoor enclosure with the "cage furniture" in place. Jackson's chameleons can be obtained directly from breeders and chameleon ranchers at herpetocultural trade shows, ordered from breeders through herpetocultural magazines, or purchased from pet shops. The other option is to take a vacation to Hawaii and collect your own.

When purchasing a Jackson's chameleon, it is best if you can observe several specimens first and make the selection yourself. *Never* purchase any chameleon that is listless, has sunken eyes, is extremely lightweight, will not feed in front of you, or shows any signs of damage to its mouth or feet. Such an animal will probably not survive for more than a few days at most. (The normal life span for a captive Jackson's chameleon maintained in both indoor and outdoor enclosures as outlined in this article is 3 to 8 years.)

The seller should allow you to carefully select the lizard you want. Place your hand in front of and underneath the chameleon so that it can crawl onto your hand. Never pull a chameleon off a branch by grabbing it by the body, as you may injure one of its feet or rip off a toenail.

Once the chameleon is in your hand, you may gently cup your hand around its body to hold and examine it. The chameleon will not like to be restrained in this manner (normally you would only let it crawl on you and not hold it in this way). As a result, it will gape (open its mouth). Look at the inside of the mouth to make sure that it does not look infected or that the edge is not damaged or dark and crusty. When you return the chameleon to the enclosure, notice whether it uses all four feet, and whether both eyes are open and working. Look to be sure that the vent opening is not inflamed. The chameleon should look alert, not listless. There should be no rips or tears on its skin. No signs of runny feces should be present in its enclosure or on the underside of its tail.

Before making a final selection of any lizard, always have a magnifying glass with you. Pull it out of your pocket and look more closely at any area of the lizard in question. Also be sure to look over its entire body with the magnifying glass for signs of mites or other external parasites. If you see mites, pass on every chameleon at that place and make your selection elsewhere.

How well you make your initial inspection before purchase will probably determine whether your pet will give you with a great deal of long-term joy or bring you quick sadness. Sick chameleons generally do not survive, even with good (and expensive) care from a veterinarian.

Initial Things to Do

When you bring your Jackson's chameleon home, first weigh it on a gram scale. The lizard can be placed into a small container to be weighed. (Be sure to subtract the weight of the container.) When recording its weight, enter the weight onto a data sheet for each of your chameleons. You should weigh each lizard at monthly intervals, or at any other time they look substantially thinner or heavier than normal. Such data can help you determine whether or not an animal might be gravid, is feeding properly, or may be ill.

If you work closely with a reptile veterinarian, a fresh stool sample can be placed in a plastic bag and taken to the vet by pre-arrangement. Be sure that your vet is in and on duty. A nonreptile vet probably will do you little good. The sample must be examined when it is fresh. The purpose of a stool sample is to check for various types of worms (internal parasites) that may be present. These can usually be eliminated easily through the use of an appropriate *oral* parasiticide prescribed by an experienced reptile vet.

Refer to the chapter on diseases and syndromes for a better understanding of the types of medical conditions that may occur in chameleons.

Care in Captivity

There are several management regimes suitable for various broad categories of chameleons. The Jackson's chameleon is a mid-elevation, arboreal, cool-tropical climate, montane species and a generalized feeder. The management recipe outlined will work well for Jackson's and most species of chameleons that fall under this montane category. Remember that they need to be housed individually unless the enclosure is extremely large and well planted. Never house more than one male to an enclosure, no matter how large the enclosure is.

It is essential that anyone wishing to keep Jackson's chameleons plan on having either a large screened enclosure on rollers or one "indoor enclosure" and one "outdoor enclosure" for each chameleon or group of chameleons. Of course, if you are so fortunate as to live in an ideal climate for them, such as Hawaii or a beach city in coastal California, then you only need one enclosure, an "outdoor enclosure."

Male Jackson's chameleon (*Chamaeleo jacksonii*). Photo by Sean McKeown.

Female Jackson's chameleon *(Chamaeleo jacksonii xantholophus)*. Photo by Sean McKeown.

The Indoor Enclosure

The indoor enclosure must have a vertical format. This is most important because your goal is not to adapt your Jackson's chameleon to a cage, but rather to select or build your enclosure to meet the specific needs of your Jackson's chameleon. Always house individuals indoors singly. The indoor enclosure can be screen, welded wire mesh, or glass (screen is preferable). Ideally, the enclosure should be roomy and well ventilated; use plastic rather than wire screening so that the screen is nonabrasive. The *minimum* dimensions for an indoor, plexiglass, commercially produced, hexagonal enclosure for one chameleon is a 21-inch (53-cm) diameter by a $19\,^1/_2$-inch (50-cm) height. The larger enclosure you can use, however, the better.

Very serviceable screened enclosures can be easily and cheaply built, purchased at reptile trade shows, or ordered through dealers who advertise in herpetocultural magazines such as *The Vivarium, Reptile and Amphibian* and *Reptiles.* Screened enclosures generally are reasonably priced. They can be readily and quite cheaply obtained in a little larger than minimum size, such as a rectangular enclosure 3 feet (90 cm) high by 2 feet (60 cm) wide by 2 feet (60 cm) long. Screened enclosures give the advantage of additional air circulation, which is highly beneficial to a Jackson's chameleon. Ideally, use as large a screened enclosure as you have room for and can afford.

The substrate (material on the enclosure bottom) should be either newspaper cut to the desired shape and size *or* several inches of good-quality topsoil. A potted bush such as a fig (*Ficus benjamina*) should take up most of the inside of the enclosure and should be pruned of small branches that could inhibit the chameleon's movement over the bulk of the small tree.

Lighting

The top portion of the enclosure should be a screen or welded wire mesh (never glass) and should have a fluorescent light fixture resting on it. Ideally you should use one UV-A (BL type black light) and one high UVB full spectrum tube (such as ZooMed, ReptaSun UVB310 or ESU Daylight Bulb). For example, use one ESU Daylight Bulb and one BL-type blacklight, or similar products now on the market and advertized in herpetoculture magazines. Generally, these bulbs need to be replaced at 6-month intervals to get maximum output. At another portion of the screen top, place a porcelain-base aluminum reflector hood, and use a 40-to-60-watt incandescent bulb, spotlight, or plant-grow bulb for *basking* use. A three-prong outlet plug is recommended and should be plugged into a safety bar (available at any hardware store) for fire prevention. Also purchase a timer for the lights and provide a consistent daily photoperiod of 12 to 14 hours of light each day.

All chameleons benefit from good air flow. Remember that Jackson's chameleons do not like—and *will quickly perish in*—hot, stuffy, low-airflow, constant-temperature enclosures.

Desired Indoor Enclosure Temperatures

The ideal temperature is 77° F (25° C) during the day and 62° F (17° C) at night, with a basking spot of 85° F (29° C); however, exact temperatures are not as critical with chameleons as is a suitable temperature range or gradient. A suitable daytime indoor range is 75 to 79° F (24 to 25° C), with perching areas (branches) in the enclosure that provide the chameleons with the opportunity to bask under a 40-to-60-watt bulb. Make sure, however, that the chameleon cannot touch the bulb. The nighttime temperature should be in the 60s° F (16 to 21° C). If possible, a minimum day-to-night difference of 10° F (5° C) is highly desirable. Do *not* use hot rocks, heating pads, or heat tapes with these arboreal lizards.

Watering and Humidity

The live plants and earth substrate should be watered each day to provide *moderate*, not high, humidity. If the earth substrate is properly watered, the soil should be dry by the next morning. An ideal relative humidity range for Jackson's chameleons is 50 to 75 percent.

Watering Your Chameleon(s)

Most species of chameleons, including Jackson's, have substantial water requirements (DeVosjoli, 1990). Most Jackson's chameleons will not drink from a water bowl; rather, they need simulated rain. You can achieve this either by spraying a fine stream of water at the edge of the mouth of a chameleon using a spray bottle to incite it to drink and/or using an overhead drip system on a timer. The simplest way to create a drip system is to use a plastic (delicatessen) cup with a pinhole in the bottom. Be sure that a similar-size or slightly larger receptacle is present directly underneath, at the bottom of the enclosure, to collect the water. Do not allow the enclosure bottom to become excessively wet as a result of improper placement of your water-collection container. This will create stuffy, moldy conditions that are unhealthy for your chameleon and can cause respiratory and dermatological problems (Jenkins, 1992). Empty the water collection container daily. It is generally best to water the chameleon once and to mist the plants once a day or twice each day.

Small Children, Dogs, Cats, and Parrots

Wild animals of any sort find it stressful to encounter potential predators and quick movements. Your chameleons should be placed only in quiet, peaceful settings. Their indoor enclosure should be in rooms or other areas that are off limits to all but chameleon-friendly, endothermic friends and family members.

The Outdoor Enclosure

If you want to keep a Jackson's chameleon, it is your responsibility to have an outdoor enclosure for it. The enclosure can take several forms. If you live in an apartment or a condominium, the enclosure can be placed on your patio or lanai. If you live in a house, the outdoor enclosure can be built in your yard around a bush that gets morning sun and that affords your chameleon some shade in the afternoon. Ornamental citrus trees make ideal chameleon outdoor habitat over which you can build a hardware wire (heavy screen) cover. Use $1/4$-inch (6-mm) hardware wire with a wood frame. Have a well-latched and lockable door on one side, large enough to allow you to reach any spot in the enclosure. In extremely warm climates such as those of Florida, Georgia, or Hawaii, build the enclosure around a bush that gets morning sun only and is shielded by a building from afternoon sun. In the midwest or eastern United States, build the enclosure around a bush that gets both morning and afternoon sun. Be sure that the vegetation of any bush is heavy enough to provide sun, shade, and a thermal gradient.

Outdoor Enclosure Watering

Watering can be as simple as spraying the top of the enclosure with a hose for 30 to 60 seconds twice each day when the weather is sunny, or as moving a sprinkler to hit a portion of the enclosure. The sprinkler can even be set on a timer. In very warm climates, a constant-drip system must be attached to the top of the enclosure to help cool the air whenever the temperature rises to 90° F (31° C) or higher. Be sure to use $1/_4$-inch (6-mm) hardware wire rather than plastic screening for the perimeter barrier of the outdoor enclosure to keep out cats, raccoons, opossums, and other potential predators. A latch with a small lock is also useful to discourage the impulse-oriented chameleon rustler.

The frame of an outdoor enclosure may be square, rectangular, or circular. The reason that an outdoor enclosure is necessary is that your Jackson's chameleon needs as much outside time as you can give it when the weather is suitable. Anytime the air temperature is between 55 and 89° F (between 13 and 32° C), your Jackson's chameleon can be outside during the day. Anytime the daytime temperature is in that range and the nighttime temperature does not drop below 40° F (4° C), your Jackson's chameleon can remain out at night as well. This species of montane lizard thrives on temperature variation. No matter where you live in the United States, there are many days during the warm months when your lizard can be out all the time. There are periods of several hours during the week, even in cooler climates, when it is sunny enough during the late fall, winter, and early spring that your chameleon can go out for portions of the day. In these cool climates, a few hours on weekends work well if you are home to monitor weather conditions. Jackson's chameleons have a need to bask using natural sunlight and respond extremely well to good airflow. The outdoor time your chameleon gets will help keep it healthy, will allow it to digest its food more effectively, and, in human (anthropomorphic) terms, will also help keep its mind and body "well toned."

The best article I have ever read on the subject of keeping chameleons in captivity was written by Robert Buckley in the Vol. 3 (3) issue of *The Vivarium* magazine. Buckley points out that all Old World chameleons fare best when maintained in a state of "loose" captivity that allows them to sun themselves, feed, and drink naturally (Buckley, 1990). Essentially, the article emphasized that for a large part of the year, Jackson's chameleons can be housed outdoors in habitat tree enclosures. Each enclosure used an 18-inch- (46-cm-) high circular plastic barrier around its bottom edges with attached mesh netting. The netting must be small enough so that chameleons cannot squeeze through it. This netting over the trees effectively keeps out birds and cats. Special feeding stations and misting systems are also employed. Buckley points out that in addition to saving you money on electrical bills, chameleons living from half to most of the year outside, depending on your climate, are exposed to yearly temperature and photoperiod cycles. Their health and longevity is maintained and enhanced, and their natural reproductive cycles are maximized. The lesson here is be creative and think big when it comes to outdoor chameleon enclosures.

Food and Dietary Supplements

Jackson's chameleons are insectivorous. They feed on insects and other invertebrates. The food should be an appropriate size for your chameleon, depending on whether it is a juvenile or an adult. Neonates (newborns) will readily eat flightless (vestigial-winged) fruit flies *(Drosophila)* and hatchling to one-week-old (first-stage) crickets. Juvenile and adult chameleons should be offered as much variety in their diet as possible. Crickets are a good base food and should make up at least 50 percent of the diet. Commercially available insects such as waxworms (larvae and adult moths), butter worms, giant mealworms *(Zophobas)*, and regular mealworms *(Tenebrio)* should occasionally be supplemented. Most of these insects can be cultured easily at home as well. Right after mealworms shed, they are white in color, and this is the best time to offer them. Additionally, a sweep net in a vacant field may yield other tasty, relatively soft-bodied insects such as grasshoppers, butterflies, katydids, and cockroaches. These and small garden snails can also be fed if they are free of pesticides and snail bait. Netted honey bees can be pinned, their stingers can be cut off with small scissors; these de-venomized insects will be relished by your chameleon.

Another feeding trick is to place a trimmed piece of meat and fat from your dinner plate near some shrubbery in your backyard during the spring, late summer, or early fall. Flies will gather on the meat. If you quickly place a butterfly net over the meat, the flies will fly to the top of the net. Work one hand up the outside of the net until only a several-inch portion is above your hand. Invert the contents into a clear plastic bag. Tie it off and place it in the refrigerator. Remember to check the bag at 20-second intervals. In less than a minute, the flies will be immobilized. They can be dumped onto a piece of newspaper on the table. With a small scissor, cut off the wing on one side only. They are now ready to be emptied into the chameleon enclosure, where they will be relished by your chameleon.

If your outdoor enclosure is built around a large flowering bush, your chameleon can catch most of its own food during those warmer parts of the year when many insects are present and may need to be only supplementally fed. Observe its feeding efforts, weight, and appearance when making such a decision.

An outdoor enclosure on a patio or lanai can usually provide the natural, unfiltered sunlight that chameleons need. Commercially-raised insects should be very lightly "dusted" in a clear plastic bag or plastic jar with a vitamin and mineral powder and a vitamin D_3 source once a week. Shake the container to thoroughly spread the powder onto the insects before offering them to the chameleons. Many such products for reptiles are available at large pet shops in your area, through herpetoculture magazine advertisements, or at reptile trade shows.

It is vitally important that the feeder insects are fed nutritious, balanced diets including alfalfa, whole grain cereal like uncooked oatmeal, and fresh leafy and yellow or red-colored vegetables so that they have a good nutritional balance before being fed to the chameleon. Jackson's chameleons can develop a vitamin A deficiency if not given a good carotene source. *Gut-loading* is a term used for beefing up purchased crickets for a day or two before they are offered to animals (De Vosjoli, 1994). Professional chameleon breeders also add calcium carbonate or calcium lactate along with multiple vitamins containing vitamin D_3 to the nutritionally balanced cricket diet.

Courtship and Breeding

One of the greatest joys for a chameleon owner is to breed Jackson's chameleons. The fact that this species is live-bearing makes the process much easier because a nesting site for the female is unnecessary, and there are no eggs that need to be incubated within a specific temperature and humidity range. Courtship and breeding of the chameleons are best attempted in your outdoor enclosure. Most breeders introduce the female into the male's enclosure. The color of the female's body will indicate when she is ready to mate. A receptive female usually turns all green or all grayish green and allows the male to approach. He signals his intent by making a series of lateral head-bobbing moves, puffing up, and showing his profile to the female. Male yellow-crested Jackson's (C. j. xantholophus) show yellows and blues in their courtship coloration. If the female still appears responsive, the male moves behind the female and mounts her from above. One of his hemipenes is inserted into her cloacal opening. Actual copulation takes from 5 to 30 minutes.

A nonreceptive female will show stress colors and will be mottled with charcoal-gray and black shades in her pattern. If approached by the male, a nonreceptive female also may demonstrate aggressiveness, including gaping, hissing, and rocking from side to side; if approached even closer, she sometimes attempts to bite. If you see that the female is nonreceptive, immediately remove her back to her own enclosure and try the introductions again at monthly intervals.

After a successful mating is completed and the two lizards have moved away from each other, the female can be returned to her regular enclosure.

If the female is gravid (pregnant), she will gain weight and take on a very robust appearance over a period of several months. Once it is clear that she is gravid, it is best to house her separately. Also, you should build an inner enclosure liner of nonabrasive plastic screening and place it inside the hardware wire outer enclosure. The purpose of this is to prevent the newborn babies from crawling out of the enclo-

Jackson's chameleon catching prey. Photo by Sean McKeown.

sure through the $\frac{1}{4}$-inch hardware wire barrier. *A lost chameleon is rarely recaptured.*

The gestation period for Jackson's chameleons is 5 to 10 months, depending partially on the temperatures to which females are exposed. Chameleons are thought to be able to store sperm, a useful technique in some reptiles and one that increases the opportunities to produce offspring among relatively low-density species (Atsatt, 1953).

While she is gravid, a female may spend more time basking and may increase her food intake until the very last stages of her pregnancy. At this point, she may decrease the number of insects she consumes or even go off feed, while continuing to bask, often at several angles. If she is housed primarily indoors, be sure that a basking light is present above the enclosure. From one to several days before the actual birth, the female will become restless and move about throughout the enclosure.

The Birthing Process

The birth process typically takes place during the morning. As the female crawls along the branches, each neonate or small groups of neonates, encased in its own membrane, drops from her cloaca to the ground below. This process stimulates the neonates to emerge out of the membrane. If a baby does not immediately emerge from the membrane, try gently picking it up and dropping it a second time from the same height to stimulate it to break through its sac. It is possible that several stillborn young or infertile ova (yolks) may be released during the birthing process (DeWitt, 1988).

Juveniles and Their Care

The number of young produced by an individual female Jackson's chameleon can be between 5 and 50. Generally, older and larger females produce larger numbers of young. The complete birth process may last from 30 minutes to 8 hours. In the wild, the young would quickly disperse after being born. To simulate nature as closely as possible, separate the female parent from the newborns as soon as it is clear through your observations that her birthing process is complete. If you leave the neonates in the same enclosure, the female might eat them. The postpartum female should be offered insect food within several hours after she completes the birth process. She will have an extra large appetite for the first couple of weeks after the young are born. Be sure to heavily dust the insects fed to her with a vitamin/mineral powder and vitamin D_3 during this crucial period. Unlike some individuals of egg-laying taxa, female Jackson's chameleons normally survive the birth process if properly managed afterwards.

The newborns are a charcoal-gray or brown color with off-white striping, barring and spotting. The only portion of them capable of turning a bright color at this age is the throat area. Should a neonate become stressed, its throat may turn purplish-red. Newborn C. j. *xantholophus* typically have three very tiny horns. Neonates have a total length of about $1\,^1/_2$ to $1\,^3/_4$ inches (38 to 44 mm) and usually weigh about 0.02 ounce (0.5 g). They are ready to feed within hours of their birth, although initially they are rather clumsy at capturing prey. With practice, they become efficient insect predators.

Some breeders raise juveniles individually on sticks in plastic ice buckets, while others prefer to raise them in small groups in screened enclosures with several plants or bushes to provide climbing cover and individual territory. The young will readily take a variety of invertebrate prey. Vestigial-winged Drosophila and hatchling crickets can be cultured as ideal primary food sources. Feed small juvenile chameleons dusted insects daily. Each juvenile will need to consume about 6 to 12 small insects per daily feeding.

Mist them several times a day. Juveniles can be misted as they are chewing on an insect during feeding, but do not fill the entire mouth cavity with water. This will decrease the chance of the juvenile lizard's accidentally choking. Also, do not expose small juveniles to temperature extremes, as their body mass at this age is much less than that of adults. They can overheat and desiccate surprisingly quickly.

The juveniles generally double their size every couple of months. At 3 to 4 months of age, more adult-like color change capabilities and patterns begin to appear, and males begin developing their horns. Coloring capabilities can occur more quickly in males than in females. Adult-like colors in young females may take 6 to 10 months to develop. If you are housing juveniles in groups, be sure to separate any individuals that do not grow as quickly. Young should only be housed with siblings of similar size, so some mixing and matching will probably be necessary. As the juveniles grow, "enclosure furniture" in the form of appropriate-size live plants, as well as progressively larger insects, are necessary.

Enclosure Cleanliness

Enclosure cleanliness and good hygiene are *critical* to success. The enclosure should be clean and fresh-smelling at all times. If paper is used for substrate, it will need to be changed about three times weekly. If earth is used for substrate, have a special slotted spoon on hand to remove fecal matter each day.

Handling

No Old World chameleon likes to be excessively handled. Excessive handling may dramatically reduce its life span, although occasional handling is acceptable. Males of this species seem to be more tolerant of handling than the females. Males that are less shy seem to adjust best to occasional handling. The proper way to handle a Jackson's chameleon is to let it crawl onto your hand. Do not restrain its movements. It may wish to crawl up and rest on your shoulder or nearby on the arm of your chair or couch. When returning it to its enclosure, place your hand under a branch so that it can climb up onto it.

A female Jackson's chameleon presenting a defensive posture. Photo by Sean McKeown.

Summary

Jackson's chameleons have specialized captive care requirements. When properly managed, they are relatively long-lived and will reproduce in captivity. Proper enclosures and temperature gradients are critical to successful care and breeding.

Acknowledgments

The author wishes to thank Wendy McKeown for her keen observations and insights about Jackson's chameleons in the field in Hawaii and in captivity. The author also extends his appreciation to Gary Ferguson for reviewing the manuscript and to Bob Buckley, Todd Risley, and Cheryl DeWitt for sharing their techniques for managing and breeding Jackson's chameleons in captivity.

Literature Cited

Atsatt, S.R. 1953. "Storage of Sperm in the Female Chameleon *Microsaura pumila pumila.*" *Copeia* 1953(1): 59.

Boulenger, G.A. 1896. "Description of a new Chameleon from Uganda." *Ann. & Mag. N. Hist. Ser.* 6(17): 376.

Buckley, R. 1990. "Experiments with Habitat Trees: Notes on the Captive Management of Chameleons." *The Vivarium*, 3(3): 10-29.

Bustard, H.R. 1958. "Use of Horns by *Chamaeleo jacksoni.*" *Brit. J. Herpet.* 2: 105-107.

DeWitt, C. 1988. "Jackson's Chameleons, *Chamaeleo jacksoni*: Captive Behavior, Care and Breeding." *The Vivarium* 1(2): 17-20.

De Vosjoli, P. 1990. *The General Care and Maintenance of True Chameleons - Part 1.* Advanced Vivarium Systems, Inc. Lakeside, CA. 36 pp.

De Vosjoli, P. 1994. *The Lizard Keeper's Handbook.* Advanced Vivarium Systems, Inc. Lakeside, CA. 175 pp.

Eason, P., G.W. Ferguson and J. Hebrard. 1988. "Variation in *Chamaeleo jacksonii* (Sauria, Chamaeleontidae): Description of a New Subspecies." *Copeia* 1988(3): 580-590.

Ferguson, G.W., J. Murphy, and R. Hudson. 1990. "The Quest for the Mount Kenya Muriyu." *The Vivarium*, 3(1): 18-38.

Glaw, F., and M. Vences. 1994. *A Fieldguide to the Amphibians and Reptiles of Madagascar. Second Edition.* Köln, Germany: Moos Druck, Leverkusen and FARBO. pp. 231-257.

Hillenius, D. 1959. "The Differentiation Within the Genus *Chamaeleo* Laurenti 1768." *Beaufortia* 8: 1-92.

Jenkins, J.R. 1992. "Husbandry and Diseases of Old World Chameleons." *Journ. of Small Exotic Animal Medicine* 1(4): 166-171.

McKeown, S. 1978. *Hawaiian Reptiles and Amphibians.* Honolulu: Oriental Publishing Co. pp. 32-33.

McKeown, S. 1991. "Jackson's Chameleons in Hawaii Are the Recently Described Mt. Kenya Subspecies, *Chamaeleo jacksonii xantholophus.*" *Bull. Chicago Herp. Soc.* 26(3): 49.

Rand, A.S. 1958. "A New Subspecies of *Chamaeleo jacksonii* Boulenger and a Key to the Species of Three-horned Chameleons." *Mus. Comp. Zool. Breviora* 99: 1-8.

continued

Rand, A.S. 1961. "A Suggested Function of the Ornamentation of East African Forest Chameleons." *Copeia* 1961(4): 411-414.

Zug, G.R. 1993. *Herpetology: An Introductory Biology of Amphibians and Reptiles.* San Diego: Academic Press, Inc. pp.413-415.

À 17 inch male panther chameleon from Ambanja. Photo by John Tashjian, courtesy of Gary Ferguson.

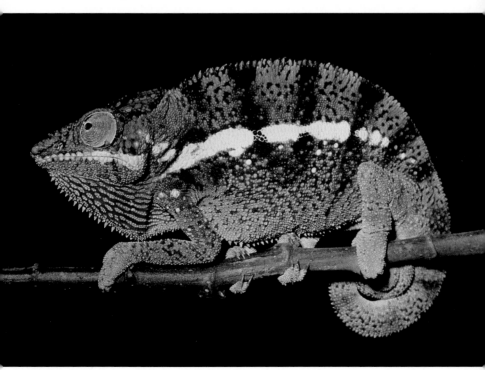

Male panther chameleon. Photo by John Tashjian, courtesy of Gary Ferguson.

Male panther chameleon from Nosy Bé photographed in the field. This animal shows the typical coloration of this local variety. Photo by Gary Ferguson.

Male panther chameleon from Diego Suarez. Photo by Bill Love.

Left: Female panther chameleon from Ambanja. Photo by Bill Love.

Nonreceptive female panther chameleon from Nosy Bé, photographed in the field. Photo by Gary Ferguson.

Female panther chameleon from Reunion Island. Photo by John Tashjian, courtesy of Chaffee Zoological Gardens.

"Blue phase" male from Nosy Bé. Photo by John Tashjian.

Color change in displaying panther chameleon from the east coast of Madagascar; initial coloration.
Photo by Gary Ferguson.

The same animal two minutes later. Photo by Gary Ferguson.

A setup for raising individual panther chameleon hatchlings. Full-spectrum lighting is placed above goldfish bowls. Photo by Gary Ferguson.

Male Jackson's chameleon (*Chamaeleo jacksonii xantholophus*). Photo by Dennis Sheridan.

Female Jackson's chameleon *(Chamaeleo jacksonii xantholophus)*. Photo by Bill Love.

Close-up of the head of a female Jackson's chameleon. Photo by Dennis Sheridan.

A pair of Jackson's chameleons photographed in the field on Oahu, Hawaii. Photo by Sean McKeown.

Newborn Jackson's chameleon photographed on Oahu, Hawaii. Photo by Sean McKeown.

Male veiled chameleon *(Chamaeleo calyptratus)*. Photo by John Tashjian.

The landscaping of a vivarium, lighting and intraspecies interaction can lead to brighter coloration in adult male veiled chameleons. Photo by Bill Love.

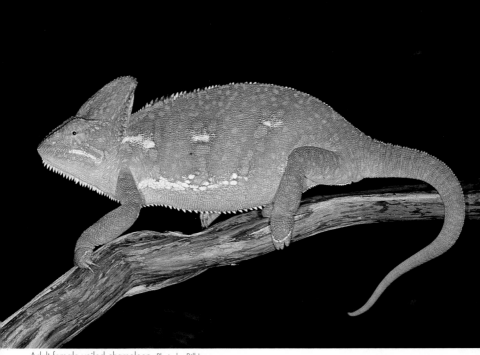

Adult female veiled chameleon. Photo by Bill Love.

Gravid female veiled chameleon showing characteristic coloration. Photo by Bill Love.

A veiled chameleon hatching. Photo by Jim Bridges and Bob Prince.

Hatchling veiled chameleon. This species grows rapidly and may reproduce by the age of six months. Photo by Dennis Sheridan.

Left: Veiled chameleon feeding. Photo by John Tashjian.

Adult male Parson's chameleon *(Chamaeleo parsonii)*. Photo by Bill Love.

An older specimen with pronounced rostral processes. Photo by John Tashjian.

Male yellow-lip morph of Parson's chameleons. Photo by Bill Love.

Female Parson's chameleon. Photo by Bill Love.

Male yellow-lip morph of Parson's chameleon drinking. These chameleons require regular watering through a drip system. Photo by Bill Love.

Close-up of head of female Parson's chameleon. Photo by Dennis Sheridan.

Part III

Veiled Chameleon
(Chamaeleo calyptratus)
Natural History, Captive Management, and Breeding

John M. Annis II

General Morphology

Note: the term *morphology* refers to the appearance or shape of animals and plants. Two major subspecies of *Chamaeleo calyptratus* have been formally identified to date. These are: *C. calyptratus calyptratus* (figure 1) and *C. calyptratus calcarifer* (figure 2). Their primary distinguishing feature is their *casque* (the general area on top of their head just behind their eyes). Males and females of both subspecies have a large cranial fin forming their casque. The *C. c. calyptratus* subspecies has a higher cranial fin, while the *C. c. calcarifer* subspecies

Figure 1. Large *Chamaeleo c. calyptratus* with slightly different coloration.
Owner Reptile Specialties.

Figure 2. Subspecies *Chamaeleo c. calcarifer* (adult male).
Photo from Hillenius & Gasperetti, 1984.

has a smaller cranial fin height (also referred to as *casque height*) as shown in figures 3a and 3b respectively. The male *C. c. calyptratus* casque height (height of cranial fin as measured from the corner of the mouth to the tip of the fin) can reach a height ranging from 68 to 107.8 mm (2.7 to 4.3 in.). The male *C. c. calcarifer* casque can reach a height ranging from 49 to 58 mm (1.9 to 2.3 in.). The female casque heights of these two subspecies range from 50 to 59 mm (2 to 2.3 in.) for *C. c. calyptratus* and from 45 to 52 mm (1.8 to 2.0 in.) for *C. c. calcarifer* (Analysis of data from Hellenius & Gasperetti, 1984). This large cranial fin is unique to chameleon species native to the Arabian peninsula and may be an important adaptation. One school of thought holds that it is used to collect condensing moisture droplets from the morning fog, which are then channeled into the corner of the animal's mouth by way of the *occipital flaps* (movable flaps along the bottom two-thirds of the back edges of the cranial fin). Another possibility is that this fin may be used to help cool the animal during the hot summer months. It would be interesting to see if there is a high density of blood vessels in the cranial fin area that could be used to cool the animal's blood and therefore lower its body temperature.

Males and females of both subspecies are *sexually dimorphic* (sexes differ in appearance or form). This dimorphism manifests itself in four areas: (1) the males typically possess a larger casque height than the females although this difference is less pronounced in *C. c. calcarifer*,

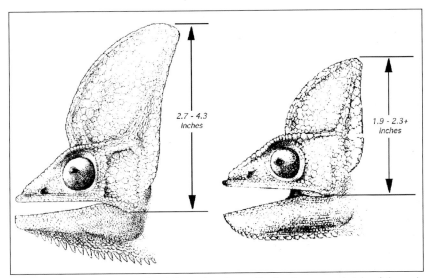

Figure 3a. Larger casque height of the male   Figure 3b. Smaller casque height of the male
Chamaeleo c. calyptratus.   Chamaeleo c. calcarifer.

Both adapted from Hillenius, 1966 (original drawings by A. Mastro).

(2) the males of both subspecies have a protrusion or "*spur*" on their hind heels (as shown in figure 10 on page 96) that does not occur in the females of either subspecies, (3) adult males and females of both subspecies display differing color patterns, and (4) the males of both subspecies generally have a greater total body length. Total head+body+tail length of the two subspecies are thought to be close; however, data from Hellenius & Gasperetti (1984) suggests *C. c. calcarifer* may be smaller. A male *C. calyptratus* can reach an adult length of approximately 17 to 24 inches (43.1 to 61 cm) from tip of snout to tip of fully extended tail (tail length ranging from 8.9 to 12.6 inches or 22.6 to 32 cm) and a weight of about 90 to 180 gm (3.2 to 6.3 oz). Female *C. calyptratus* can reach a head+body+tail length of approximately 10 to 13 inches or 25.4 to 33 cm (tail length from 5.7 to 7.2 inches or 14.5 to 10.2 cm) and a *midterm* weight (animal weight midway through egg development, as females always contain developing eggs) of about 90 to 120 gm or 3.2 to 4.2 ounces.

Color patterns of both *C. calyptratus* subspecies are reported to be highly variable even within the same clutch. Male *C. c. calyptratus* typically have light yellow or gold bands with orange fringes alternating with grass-green bands. The *ventral* (underside) and *gular* (throat) areas are typically a light blue-green with dark blue-green spots. Horizontal rows of white patches with dark edges may also be displayed laterally and occur on males and females of both *C. c. calyptratus* and

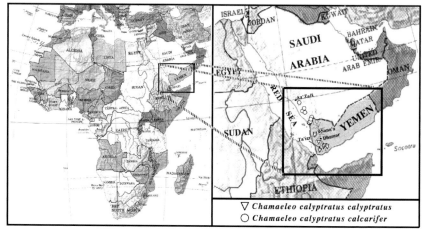

Figure 4. Rectangular area showing overall range of *Chamaeleo calyptratus* in Yemen and in Southern Arabia (ranges of *Chamaeleo c. calyptratus* & *Chamaeleo c. calcarifer* marked as triangles and circles respectively). Species locations adapted from Hillenius & Gasperetti, 1984.

C. c. calcarifer. Males of the *C. c. calcarifer* subspecies have grass-green bands with dark broken patches alternating against silver or light-yellow bands with dark spots. The tail of the *C. c. calcarifer* is slightly thinner.

Range

Off the northeastern corner of the African continent, across the Red Sea, and on the southern half of the Arabian Peninsula lie southern Saudi Arabia and Yemen, home of *C. calyptratus*. This species of chameleon is found in western Yemen and southern Saudi Arabia. It inhabits primarily the west slopes of a mountain range that starts at *Ta'izz* and extends north along the west coast of the peninsula through *Dhamar*, up through *Sana'a* (the capital of Yemen), and into Saudi Arabia. *C. calyptratus* is also prevalent on the mountain slopes off the southern tip of the peninsula in south Yemen (figure 4). A review of documented sightings (Hillenius & Gasperetti, 1984; Meerman & Boomsma, 1987) shows that *C. c. calyptratus* occurs in the rain-fed mountain slopes of southwest and southern Yemen and in the drier central high plateau regions farther north around *Dhamar* and west of *Sana'a*, while *C. c. calcarifer* occurs primarily on the drier plains and plateaus along the southwestern coast of Saudi Arabia. Figure 4 gives a graphic representation of these localities.

Habitat

 C. calyptratus habitat can be divided into roughly three distinct types: (1) the humid low coastal plains of Yemen and south Saudi Arabia, (2) the rain-fed western and southern mountain slopes of south Yemen, (3) the high plateaus of north Yemen and southern Saudi Arabia. Yemen has a narrow coastal plain bordering the Red Sea that continues northward into Saudi Arabia. Here it is extremely humid with average daytime temperatures ranging from 86° F (30° C) in January to 110° F (43.3° C) in July. Rainfall seldom exceeds 4 inches (10.2 cm) per year. This narrow coastal plain rises steeply to a mountainous interior, and in Yemen reaches altitudes above 12,000 feet (3,658 m) near *Sana'a*. Because of this, moisture evaporated from the Red Sea in the form of clouds hits these mountains and is forced upwards to higher altitudes, where the cooler air causes these clouds to condense, forming rain. The Southern mountain slopes of Yemen are an exceptional part of Arabia, receiving moderate to abundant rainfall between March and September (nearly half the year). At *Ibb*, a town just north of *Ta'izz*, the mountains may receive more than 80 inches (2.03 m) of rainfall per year. As a result, although most of this area has been cultivated to grow corn, millet, coffee, and dates, semilush vegetation and its associated insect life are abundant, providing more than adequate conditions for *C. c. calyptratus* to thrive. Average daytime temperatures are milder, ranging from 68° F (20° C) in January to 86° F (30° C) in July, and it is less humid than the low coastal plains. Intermediate between the two extremes of the low coastal plains and rain-fed mountain slopes are the drier high plateaus, which lie around *Dhamar* just west of *Sana'a* and farther north into Saudi Arabia. Here there is an almost treeless landscape with no more than 20 inches (50.8 cm) of rainfall per year. With the help of irrigation, however, additional crops are grown. In these high plains severe night frosts can occur. It is thought that *C. calyptratus* protect themselves from the frost by climbing down and sleeping in crevices in the ground. This behavior was demonstrated by captive *C. c. calyptratus* when several wild-caught animals kept freely in a room were observed to climb down and sleep between the central heating panels and curtain folds near the floor. This behavior occurred most frequently when nightfall was accompanied by a large temperature drop (Meerman & Boomsma, 1987). This behavior has also been reported by several Chameleon Information Network (C.I.N.) members.

 Throughout the mountain slopes and high plateaus, and occasionally down into the low coastal plains, numerous *wadis* channel rainwater runoff from the mountains. (A wadi is a gully or riverbed that remains dry except during the rainy season or immediately after it rains.) Many wadis cut deep through the landscape. In some places these wadis contain water most of the year. Even when they are empty, the moist soil in and around them makes more vegetation possible. Here, it is suspected, lies the key to *C. calyptratus's* ability to survive in the more arid environments, for without vegetation there is little insect food to be had. Correlation of documented sightings (shown in figure 4) with a detailed map of the Arabian peninsula suggests that both *C. calyptratus calyptratus* in Yemen and *C. calyptratus calcarifer* in Saudi Arabia are concentrated around the large wadis, especially in the drier areas. Chameleons were sighted in the humid low coastal plain (which receives almost no rainfall) only where a main wadi emptied into the Red Sea. This may explain why one field study documented frequent sightings of *C. c. calyptratus* in areas changed by man, such as cultivated landscapes and even towns (Meerman & Boomsma, 1987), if these changes included an increase in vegetation due to irrigation and homestead landscape maintenance. Figure 3-4 shows a clear division between the ranges of *C. calyptratus calyptratus* and *C. calyptratus calcarifer* on the north western border of Yemen. It has been suggested that *C. calyptratus* evolved into two separate subspecies as a result of isolation by the mountain range in north Yemen (*Meerman & Boomsma, 1987*). This remains to be confirmed in future field studies. It seems more likely that this isolation is due to a combination of the mountain range, the essentially rainless low coastal plain, and the vast Arabian deserts to the East.

Territorial Behavior

C. calyptratus is one of the most aggressive species of chameleon known. Upon immediate sight of one another, males will display spectacularly vivid colors, flatten their rib cages, expand their gular areas (the patch of elastic skin extending from beneath the jawbone or mandibles), and stand sideways to look larger and more formidable to the rival male, while continuously swinging back and forth, nodding their heads, and curling and uncurling their tails. Figure 5 shows a young adult male with expanded gular area and curling tail. Physical encounters can be extremely violent. In the initial stages of physical confrontation, rival males will jab each other with their snouts (while keeping their mouths closed). If neither animal backs down, fierce fighting breaks out. A large adult male *C. calyptratus* has powerful jaws, and broken limbs, casques, or ribs are a common result of these bouts. The loser's light bands will turn gray, the rest of his body will turn a combination of brown, dark green, and black, and he will flee the scene. As

Figure 5. Young adult male in territorial stance. Photo courtesy of C.I.N. member Scott Shoemaker, M.D.

with most chameleon species, a younger adult will usually run the moment he catches sight of a larger full-grown adult. Although hatchlings and subadults of similar age can be placed in the same enclosure until just before sexual maturity, mature animals of either sex should not be kept together. Under ideal conditions, female *C. calyptratus* reach sexual maturity at approximately 4 to 6 months, with males reaching sexual maturity at approximately 6 months of age. It has been reported that males sit at the top of individual trees within sight of each other, with the middle portion of a tree containing cycling, gravid, and subadult females and the lower portion of the tree containing subadult males. Hatchlings remain primarily in the surrounding tall grasses. With the benefit of further behavioral study, it may be possible to keep a breeding colony of different ages and sexes together in a large enclosure, which simulates conditions that promote this behavioral model. This remains to be determined.

Temperature

C. calyptratus are intense baskers. Reports of animals basking under 50- to 100-watt incandescent reflector lamps, even when the ambient temperature is 80 to 90° F (26.2 to 32.2° C), are common. It is important, however, to make sure that basking animals do not burn themselves. This can result from basking too close to, or even coming in contact with, the incandescent light source. Because of the large nighttime temperature drop on the mountain slopes and high plateaus of their native habitat, C. *calyptratus* probably go through a warm-up cycle each morning, basking intensely in the sun to raise their body temperatures to desired levels. This basking behavior performs another important function. The sun's ultraviolet rays between the wavelengths of 290 to 315 nanometers convert 7-dehydrocholesterol in the animal's skin into D_3, a vitamin without which most animals (including man) cannot absorb calcium from their digestive tracts. Gravid females commonly exhibit increased basking behavior, especially in the final weeks before laying. This may be a way of producing additional D_3 to meet the demands of their developing eggs. It is estimated that C. *calyptratus* will begin to reach thermal stress at between approximately 110 and 120° F (43.3 and 48.9° C).

Special Adaptations

Reptiles are *uricotelic*, which means that they excrete sodium, potassium, and ammonium salts of uric acid rather then liquid urine containing urea as by-products of their protein metabolism. In environments where water must be conserved, some reptiles have evolved nasal salt glands. These glands allow the animal to excrete sodium, potassium, and chloride ions in concentrated form without losing precious water (*Frye, 1991*). Both subspecies of C. *calyptratus* possess nasal salt glands as an adaptation to environments where water may be scarce. Occasionally, white salt deposits may be seen around the nostrils of both subadult and adult captive animals.

Mating Behavior

The mating behavior of chameleons is often misinterpreted by the beginner. Although there may be many similarities across species, mating behavior is species specific and if misinterpreted can sometimes lead to disastrous results. This is especially true of *C. calyptratus*. *Passive colors* is a term used by the C.I.N. to refer to the color pattern displayed when a chameleon is in its passive state (not frightened, defending territory, or aggressively pursuing another animal, and in good health). In many species, such as *C. johnstoni* and *C. jacksonii*, the female's displaying of passive coloration in the presence of an amorous male is the main indicator of her readiness to mate. Other species, such as *C. dilepis* and *C. calyptratus*, may display distinct *mating colors*. The female passive colors of *C. calyptratus* are a light green with horizontal rows of white patches and sometimes orange or yellow elongated spots. The number and location of these spots is highly variable, even among animals of the same clutch. In this particular case, the yellow spotting is absent. The mating colors of *C. calyptratus* are the same as their passive colors with one important difference. When receptive to mating, females will usually, but not always, display light *Robin's-egg blue* markings along the back and tail with vertical streaks of the same color on the casque. Smaller blue spots will occur laterally farther down on the sides of her body. When an adult male *C. calyptratus* catches sight of a female, he will react in much the same way as he does when he catches sight of another male. He will brighten his colors, flatten his rib cage, expand his gular area, and curl his tail. He will then begin nodding his head from side to side with a quick jerking motion while approaching the female with a sort of swinging gait. If the female is receptive she will remain in her mating colors and slowly begin to crawl away. Sometimes the male will jab her on the hips with his snout while keeping his mouth closed. He will then mount the female, move his *cloaca* (an organ roughly analogous to the rectum in mammals into or through which urinary, digestive, and reproductive organs deposit their products) along either side of the female's cloaca and extend one of his *hemipenes* into the female. (The male's copulatory organs consist of two hemipenes which are stored in the tail behind the cloaca.) The act of mating lasts several minutes and may occur more than once during the day. When introducing a female into a male's enclosure for the purpose of mating, care must be taken not to disturb the male to the point that he becomes so agitated he will attack anything that enters his territory, even a receptive female. This is especially true of wild-caught males. Several C.I.N. members have reported that males injured females during an attempt to mate their animals. It is recommended that only male and female animals of similar size be placed together for mating, so that the female is able to defend herself. It may even be preferable that the female be slightly larger than the male. Once initial mating begins, the danger of aggression by the male decreases significantly; however, the mating pair should be watched closely (at least initially) for signs of undue aggression by the male and separated if necessary. Dr. Gary Ferguson of Texas Christian University recommends that male and female *C. pardalis* be kept within sight of each other for a few minutes, to allow normal courting behavior to develop, before actually placing the animals together. This technique may prove helpful with *C. calyptratus*.

On the other hand, if the female is not in a receptive state, upon immediate sight of an amorous male she will turn a dark green or black with bright blue and yellow spots, expand her gular area, curl her tail, flatten her body, and rock from side to side on her perch. If the male is close enough, she will usually gape fiercely at him. Females will begin to reject the male anywhere from 18 hours to 3 days after a successful copulation and will demonstrate this by a display of warning colors sometimes even in the presence of another female. *It is important to understand that a female who has successfully mated will display warning colors only in the presence of a male (and possibly another female) but may continue to display normal mating colors in her passive (unstressed) state.* Females will usually continue to display warning colors when they catch sight of a male until approximately 60 days following *oviposition* (egg-laying), at which point mating colors may again be displayed.

Oviposition

The females of both subspecies are *oviparous* (egg laying) rather then *ovoviviparous* (live-bearing). One of the most prolific species of chameleons known, captive female *C. calyptratus* may lay clutches ranging in size from 27 to well over 80 eggs every 90 to 120 days (3 to 4 times per year). Clutch size is proportional to the size of the parent animal, with the larger females producing the larger clutches. Egg formation within *C. calyptratus* begins when the females are less than one month old and the as yet unfertilized eggs are 30 to 50 percent developed at the time of mating. Captive female *C. calyptratus* become receptive to mating for a brief period of approximately 10 to 15 days at an incredible 3.5 to 5 months of age and again at around 60 days after each oviposition. Females that miss their first mating almost always die egg bound; it is critical that the pet owner watch closely for virgin females to display their mating colors, so as not to miss this brief period of receptivity. The C.I.N. has received several reports, however, of females mating without showing the blue coloration, displaying only their passive colors in the presence of a male (even at first mating). It might be wise, therefore, to attempt mating of virgin females if they show only their passive coloration in the presence of a male. *C. calyptratus* females store sperm and are capable of laying at least 2 consecutive fertile clutches from a single mating. As a result, except for their first time, females do not have to be mated for every clutch. Frequently, multiple clutching females that would normally be due for another mating do not show their mating colors, but instead display *warning colors* at the sight of a male and will then go on to lay a second fertile clutch before mating again. Females lay their eggs 20 to 30 days after mating (or 90 to 120 days after their last oviposition if multiple clutching from a single mating). By contrast, the clutch sizes of wild *C. calyptratus* are much smaller, ranging from 12 to 20 eggs. It is thought that some key environmental factor in their natural habitat may be responsible for regulating clutch size. This might be photoperiod, seasonal temperature fluctuation, the cyclical abundance of a certain plant or key nutrient they consume, or simply the increased abundance of food in captivity. This remains to be determined. Females in captivity rarely live beyond their fifth or sixth clutch. This may be due to the extremely large clutch size of captive animals, which averages 3 to 4 times that of wild females. It is not known how long females live in the wild, but finding the key factor(s) that control clutch size in this species (if they exist) is worth further study because it may significantly increase the lifespan of females in captivity.

Three to five days before oviposition, female *C. calyptratus* usually stop eating, become restless, possibly climbing about the cage, and linger at perch areas near the bottom of the enclosure. In the final 10 to 20 days of development, the maturing eggs account for more than half of the animal's total body weight. At oviposition, a female *C. calyptratus* will dig a tunnel at a 45-to-50-degree angle, using her front claws to loosen the soil and her back feet to move the loosened soil out of the burrow. She will then back herself almost completely into the tunnel with only her nose visible and lay her eggs very rapidly. Once all eggs have been laid, she will then turn around and pack the tunnel, again using primarily her front feet. When behavior signs indicate that the female is nearing oviposition, the female should be placed in a separate enclosure or container. The bottom of this enclosure should be lined with about 4 to 6 inches (10.2 to 15.2 cm) of beach sand moistened enough to hold a formed tunnel (but not wet). Loose moistened soil does not seem to work as well, because it does not hold a tunnel as well as sand. Interestingly, the C.I.N. has received at least two reports of females laying their eggs in tunnels dug directly under the root balls of potted plants. In the wild it may be that *C. calyptratus* tunnel under the root systems of plants or trees, where the soil is softer and easier to remove. Unlike most of the other species of Chamaeleonidae studied to date, female *C. calyptratus* recognize stray eggs and will purposefully move them into the tunnel or cover them.

Incubation of Eggs

C. calyptratus eggs are oval shaped and range in weight from 1 to 1.5 gm (.04 to .05 oz). Eggs weighing less than a gram are rarely viable. The eggs of captive animals range from about 8 to 9 mm (.3 to .35 in.) in width and from about 15 to 17 mm (.59 to .67 in.) in length. Females brought in from the wild (which are almost always carrying fertile eggs) will initially lay smaller clutches where the eggs may be slightly larger on average. Newly laid eggs can be left buried for a few hours or removed immediately after oviposition. The eggs should then be placed in a container that is partially filled with moderately moist, but not wet, vermiculite, peat moss, sphagnum moss, or perlite as incubation medium. Ron Tremper (the first to set up a large-scale breeding operation in this country for *C. c. calyptratus*) uses perlite exclusively. He recommends mixing 1.5 parts perlite with no more than 1 part water by weight. (*Important: amounts are measured by weight, not by volume.*) The container should not be filled with so much incubation medium that there is no space left for the hatchings to occupy. The eggs should then be placed on their side, partially buried in the moistened incubation medium so that 30 to 40 percent of the egg surface is exposed. Any misshapen or obviously infertile eggs should be discarded. The container opening should then be covered with a lid, or with plastic wrap secured by a rubber band with 2 or 3 pin-size holes punched in the lid (or plastic wrap). The eggs should be checked every 2 weeks. If necessary, moisture should be replenished and molding or infertile eggs discarded. If incubated at 80 to 88° F (26.7 to 31.1° C) during the day with a nightly temperature drop to a low of 74° F (23.3° C), the eggs will hatch in approximately 150 to 190 days. It is not known if, in the wild, the eggs of *C. calyptratus* (which may be buried in tunnels anywhere from 8 to 12+ inches or 20.3 to 31+ cm underground) experience temperatures as high as 88° F (31.1° C) during the day with such a large drop in the evenings. Further field study measurements are needed to determine this once and for all. In one experiment, clutches of *C. c. calyptratus* eggs were split into three groups.

Figure 6. *Chamaeleo c. calyptratus* eggs incubating close together in perlite (1.5 oz perlite mixed with 1 oz of water).

Group 1 was incubated at a temperature ranging from 80 to 88° F (26.7 to 31.1° C) during the day with a temperature drop reaching a low of 74° F (23.2° C) in the evenings. Group 2 was incubated at a constant 82° F (27.8° C), and Group 3 was incubated at a constant 92° F (33.3° C). All three groups of eggs were placed close together in 1.5 parts perlite mixed with 1 part water (by weight) in separate one-pint delicatessen cups as shown in figure 6. Group 1 (the eggs with the nightly temperature drop) hatched first, Group 2 hatched second, and Group 3 hatched last (*Tremper, personal conversation*).

Unlike some species whose eggs may hatch over several days, *C. calyptratus* hatchlings emerge from their eggs all at the same time. It is thought that this mass hatching may be a strategy designed to increase the hatchling survival rate by presenting would-be predators with many moving targets at once. If, in the wild, *C. calyptratus* eggs are buried deep in the ground, mass hatching may allow hatchlings to help each other dig their way to the surface. This remains to be determined. Interestingly, in captivity, eggs from the same clutch that are split and incubated in separate containers hatch simultaneously within a given container, but each container hatches independently of the other. This suggests that there is some sort of communication process going on among the eggs that forces them all to hatch simultaneously. In an

Figure 7. Separated *Chamaeleo c. calyptratus* eggs incubating in vermiculite (using a relatively dry $\frac{1}{4}$ cups water to $1\frac{1}{2}$ cups vermiculite).

experiment conducted by Petr Necas in Czechoslovakia (one of the first to hatch *C. calyptratus* in captivity), a clutch of *C. c. calyptratus* eggs was split into two groups and incubated in separated containers. The first group was incubated with eggs placed close together similar to figure 6. The second group was incubated under the same conditions except the eggs were placed apart from one another, similar to figure 7, but much farther apart. Eggs that were incubated together had only a 79 percent hatch rate and hatched all at once. Some of the hatchlings were smaller, ranging from 2.1 to 3.0 inches (5.3 to 7.6 cm) in length (from nose to tail tip). Eggs that were incubated apart hatched over a 27-day period, but had a 95 percent hatch rate, with hatchling size ranging from 2.6 to 3.0 inches (6.6 to 7.6 cm) in length. Two of the hatchlings from eggs incubated together died within the first month, whereas none of the hatchlings died from the eggs that were incubated separately. This suggests that the first eggs to hatch chemically signal the rest of the clutch to hatch as well. As a result, other eggs that would otherwise not be ready to hatch are forced to hatch prematurely. (The C.I.N. calls this phenomenon a *mass hatching response.*) The hatchlings that are incubated together are normally smaller and weaker. This is evidenced by the observation that the difference between the largest and smallest animals hatched from eggs incubated together is almost 0.9 inch (2.3

cm), while the difference between the largest and smallest animals hatched from eggs incubated apart was only 0.4 in. (1.0 cm).

Another experiment by Petr Necas showed that eggs subjected to daily ambient daylight had only a 37 percent hatch rate, were on average an inch smaller, and hatched 15 to 17 days earlier then other eggs (from the same clutch), that were incubated in total darkness and had an 81 percent hatch rate. These findings suggest that daylight during incubation and the mass hatching response both cause *C. c. calyptratus* eggs to hatch prematurely *(Necas, 1991)*. Hence, it is recommended that *C. calyptratus* eggs be placed no less then an inch apart from each other in the incubation medium and incubated in total darkness. Again, incubation at 80 to 88° F (26.7 to 31.1° C) during the day with a 10-to-18° F (5.6-to-10° C) temperature drop in the evenings has been used successfully; however, a cooler daytime incubation temperature may give better results. Further field measurements from the *C. calyptratus* habitat are needed to confirm the correct incubation regime.

Care of Hatchlings

When the eggs are about to hatch, they shrink slightly, and small water beads appear on the egg surfaces (often referred to as *sweating*). Twelve to 15 hours later, the hatchlings make star slits at either end of the eggs and poke their noses out just enough to breathe. In this position they will remain for another 10 to 15 hours while they pull any remaining egg yolk into their abdomen. For this reason, it is not recommended to remove hatchlings from their eggs manually. Hatchlings measure anywhere from 2.1 to 3.0 inches (5.3 to 7.6 cm) in length (from nose tip to tail tip) at hatch point and may begin eating immediately or may wait as long as 2 days. Although much less pronounced than in adult animals, with close inspection male hatchlings are distinguishable from females at birth by their hind spurs (as shown in figure 10), which the females do not possess. It is thought that a large percentage of hatchlings whose egg yolks are not completely pulled into their bodies, that are less than 2.5 inches (6.4 cm) in length, or that do not eat for 2 or 3 days are indications that factors present during incubation (such as those discussed earlier) caused the clutch to hatch prematurely. It is of key importance that C. *calyptratus* hatchlings be reared in an enclosure that has good ventilation. Although hatchlings will readily accept waxworms and mealworms, they regurgitate these food types soon after they eat them. Initially, therefore, hatchlings fare best on 2-week-old crickets, small snails, and houseflies (but not blue bottle flies), until they are about 8 inches (20.3 cm) in length.

Feeding and Supplementation

Like most chameleon species, C. *calyptratus* eat crickets, locusts, grasshoppers, flies, mealworms, snails, waxworms, spiders, and almost any type of insect presented to them. Significantly, C. *calyptratus* have been reported to consume earthworms, which have a high calcium-to-phosphorus ratio. There have been some scattered reports, however, of adult animals going off feed and dying after being fed a diet consisting primarily of super (giant) mealworms for a period of about 2.5 to 4 weeks. *C. calyptratus* grow very rapidly and require a continuous supply of feed insects. In captivity *C. calyptratus* females lay extremely large clutches and thus require extra vitamin supplementation. If animals are not allowed to bask in natural sunlight, they will require vitamin D_3 supplementation. The most frequent nutritional deficiency encountered in captive *C. calyptratus* is a vitamin D_3 deficiency resulting from the demands of the large clutch sizes typical of this species. It is important to understand that egg formation within female *C. calyptratus* begins when they are less than a month old. Consequently, they require extra supplementation to support the developing eggs in addition to their own rapid growth, even though they have not yet been mated. Because most commercially available insects are low in calcium and high in phosphorous (especially crickets), they will require calcium supplementation as well. Care should be taken so that animals are not overdosed on vitamins (especially the fat-soluble A, E, D, and K). The specific vitamin D_3 (cholecalciferol) requirements for *C. calyptratus* have not yet been experimentally determined; however, a general dosage for reptiles of 0.1 IU (0.0025 micrograms of cholecalciferol) per gram of animal weight per week has been recommended (*Merck Veterinary Manual, 1986*). It is suggested that no more than 200 percent of this dosage be administered to females with developing eggs. (Remember: a female with eggs weighs more.) Vitamin A is also important for healthy development of eyes, tissue linings, skin, and a properly functioning immune system. Adult *C. calyptratus* can safely meet their requirements without overdosing by eating plant material high in carotenoids (pre-vitamin A), such as cooked carrots, cooked sweet potatoes, or collard greens. Collard greens are also high in calcium. (Cooking or microwaving actually releases more of carotenoid pre-vitamin A from foods.) These carotenoid-rich items can simply be fed to the 2-week-old crickets before they are in turn fed to hatchling

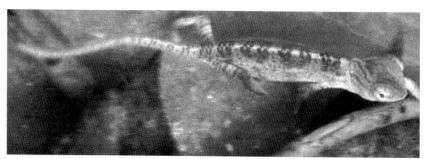

Figure 8. Two-week old *Chamaeleo c. calyptratus* hatchling caught running for cover.

Figure 9. Two-month old male *Chamaeleo c. calyptratus.*

or subadult animals. *C. calyptratus* are part of a small subset of chameleon species whose diet is composed of a significant percentage of plant matter. They will begin to eat plant material at sexual maturity and have been reported to aggressively consume a wide variety of plants and fruits. These include (but are not limited to) the leaves of pothos, philodendron, sansevieria, ficus, and collards, to name a few. They have been observed to readily consume tomatoes, peaches, bananas, tangerines, cherries, and broccoli tops. This plant-eating behavior suggests that *C. calyptratus* may have the ability to meet their water needs by absorbing moisture directly from plant material. This remains to be determined; however, it would explain how they are able to survive in parts of their range several miles from the nearest water-filled wadi, where it may not rain for years. *C. calyptratus* are truly *omnivorous* (they eat both plant material and insects) and probably other small lizards as well. Indeed, *C. calyptratus* has a much longer, more complex digestive tract than that of most other chameleons. *C. calyptratus* are also among the few species of chameleon that recognize and eat inanimate food objects, such as dead insects and even pieces of cuttlebone or calcium carbonate. They are also one of the few species that can be quickly trained to drink water out of a standing water dish. This can be accomplished by setting up a drip system, using an intravenous drip bag purchased at any hospital supply store to drip on a plastic leaf that sits in or just above a catch bowl placed at typical perch levels of animals in

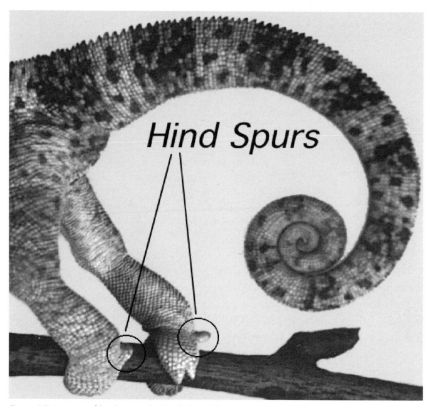

Hind Spurs

Figure 10. Location of hind spurs which only the males possess.

the cage. Eventually, they will learn to drink directly from the bowl without the drip system. *C. calyptratus* will eat its own skin sheddings, even those of other animals and may keep them in the back of its mouth for several days while it continues to eat other food normally.

Parasites

Scott Stahl D.V.M.

The most important thing to remember in dealing with parasites is that new animals should be quarantined for a minimum of 60 days, and preferably 90 days. During quarantine, note whether the animal is feeding and defecating normally, and watch for signs of illness. The longer a newly acquired animal is isolated, the greater the chance of identifying and treating a problem that might otherwise spread through the existing collection.

Nematodes (roundworms), *cestodes* (tapeworms), coccidia, flagellates, and amoeba are all common intestinal parasites of Chamaeleonidae. The most common parasites that I have found, both in wild-caught and captive-born *C. calyptratus,* are hookworms and pinworms (two types of nematodes). But tapeworms have also been identified (usually at necropsy) in several wild-caught *C. calyptratus.* Tapeworm eggs are not routinely found in feces, so it is difficult to tell by a normal fecal examination if a chameleon is harboring them. I strongly recommend several fecal examinations of each new acquisition in a pet owner's collection. All wild-caught chameleons should be *prophylactically* (preventatively) treated with *nematocidal* (anti-roundworm) and *cestocidal* (anti-tapeworm) drugs. One line of treatment that contains both a nematocide (febantel) and a cestocide (Praziquantel) is Vercom® paste. I have successfully treated chameleons with a dosage of 0.30 cc/*kg* (per kilogram of body weight), by mouth daily for three consecutive days. This drug comes in a paste form, not a liquid, so the chance of *aspiration* (being breathed into the animal's lungs) with oral administration is unlikely. For flagellates and amoebas, I commonly use metronidazole *(Flagyl®-Searle)* at a dose of 60 mg/kg orally and repeat the treatment in 2 weeks. To ensure that parasites are eliminated, several negative fecal samples are necessary.

General Comments

Of all the species of chamaeleonidae, *C. calyptratus* display some of the most spectacular colorations. Large and tenacious, they come from a climate that ranges from lush semitropical vegetation with moderate to abundant rainfall, to near desert environments. Yet they can survive where severe night frosts occur frequently. For this reason, they are able to withstand low temperatures for short periods of time. Because *C. calyptratus* are plant eaters, it is relatively easy to provide them with a balanced diet. Extremely prolific and fast growing, this species shows promise as a relatively common, easy-to-care-for animal. But this status has not been achieved yet. Much more needs to be learned about its requirements. Wild-caught and some captive-raised animals are difficult to handle and tame in captivity. Captive females lay clutches 3 to 4 times the size of wild animals and rarely survive past their fifth or sixth clutch.

Of the two subspecies discussed in here, relatively little is known about the captive requirements for *C. c. calcarifer,* although their requirements are expected to be very similar to those of *C. c. calyptratus.* On the other hand, *C. c. calyptratus* has been imported into the United States and bred extensively by importers and private pet owners for the past five years. As a result, a wealth of first-hand experience is being developed.

Literature Cited

Hillenius, D. 1966. "The Chameleons of Southern Arabia." *Beaufortia* 13: (156) 91–108.

Hillenius, D., Gasperetti, J. 1984. *Fauna of Saudi Arabia.* Vol 6, 513–526.

Meerman, J., Boomsma, L. 1987. *Samandra.* Vol 15, 11–22.

Esselte Map Service & Lidman Production AB (Sweden), 1986. *Graphic Learning Earth Book World Atlas.*

Pearce, E.A., Gordon, S. 1990. *"The Times Books World Weather Guide.*

Necas, P. 1991. *"Comments on Chamaeleo calyptratus calyptratus,"* *Herpetofauna*, 13(73), 6–9.

Necas, P. 1991. "Some Maturity Experiments on the Eggs of *Chamaeleo Calyptratus*," (Publication Unknown).

Frye, F.L. 1991. *Biomedical and Surgical Aspects of Captive Reptile Husbandry,* Krieger Pub. Vol. 1, 488.

Special Thanks to:

Ron Tremper; personal conversation and photos

Ken Kalisch; personal conversation and photo opportunities

John Uhern; personal conversation and photo opportunities

Scott Shoemaker; personal conversation and photos

Dr. Scott Stahl D.V.M.; C.I.N. advising veterinarian

Dr. William H. Gehrmann, Ph.D.; helpful suggestions

Veiled chameleon. Photo by John Tashjian.

Part IV

Herpetoculture of
The Veiled Chameleon
(Chamaeleo calyptratus)

Ronald L. Tremper
Center for Reptile and Amphibian Propagation

Introduction

This dynamic Middle Eastern species *Chamaeleo calyptratus*, the veiled chameleon, is a resident of inland river valleys (wadis) of Yemen and southern Saudi Arabia. Although veiled chameleons have been kept and bred since 1987 in what formerly was Czechoslovakia, this species was first imported into the United States during the spring of 1990.

The San Diego Zoo reported eggs laid from a captive mating in September 1990, which resulted in the first captive-bred young in the United States in March 1991. Because of private breeding efforts, numerous captive-bred young have been produced and distributed throughout the United States and Europe. Never before has there been such a chameleon that is so easily captive-bred, or so hardy, affordable, and available to the vast herpetoculture community. In my opinion, this is by far the most exciting of the chameleon species to work with because of its following attributes: large size, beautiful coloration, high reproductive potential, temperature tolerance, omnivorous diet, and 100% sexability upon hatching.

Description of Veiled Chameleons

Male veiled chameleons always have a larger body and casque (head crest) size at maturity than do females. A tarsal spur (on the "heel" of the hindlegs) is present in males at hatching, making sexing simple and accurate. Male *C. calyptratus* reach a total body length of 12 to 19 inches (30.5 to 48.3 cm) within 12 months of age. They are highly variable in color, even in specimens originating from the same clutch of eggs; the colors include bold vertical body bands of primarily bright gold, green, and blue mixed with yellow, orange, or black. Flashy bicolored or tri-colored males possessing any of these listed colors are possible. A slender body appearance is normal in mature males.

Females reach 8 to 12 inches (20.3 to 30.5 cm) total length by 12 months of age. They are usually light-green with some mottled pattern of small white-to-gold body spots and show light blue on their dorsal crest as adults. Females are more heavy bodied than males when mature. Both sexes are skittish when young and tenacious as adults, but they do tame very easily when hand-fed from forceps.

As neonates emerge from the egg they are light-green and measure 2 to 3 inches (5.1 to 7.6 cm) from nose to tail tip. Babies that appear dark in color are stressed and need suitable cover and warm caging. If you view youngsters as they sleep you can often see subtle pattern and color variations on their casques, spines and sides. Even though the young may appear to be clones, no two calyptratus are alike at maturity, thereby making it possible for anyone to hatch a one-of-a-kind wonder.

The color of *C. calyptratus* (this is particularly true of males) varies depending on the color of the foliage surrounding them. Brightly colored plants often lead a chameleon to adopt brighter-than-usual coloration.

Selection: Wild-caught or Captive-bred

"Buy smart, buy captive-bred" is always the best approach. Chameleons in nature are antisocial beasts that typically carry a heavy internal parasite load. The process of importation is a deadly mix of psychological and physical stress, aggravated by parasites. Please know that nothing has changed; wild-caught chameleons still may readily die.

The major concern in obtaining captive-bred calyptratus is their nutrition. Have the parents and young been supplemented properly? The diet varies with the breeder, but the healthy chameleon exhibits certain signs: sturdy straight limbs and jawbones are prerequisites to purchase.

Because the veiled chameleon is a new species to most collectors, and because their care requirements are vastly different from tropical species, the following list of dos and don'ts should prove useful (especially for young calyptratus).

- Keep the sexes physically and visually separate until they are 5 to 6 months old.
- Provide a 10-gallon- (38-liter-) size floor space for animals that are from 2 to 7 inches (5.1 to 17.8 cm) in total length.
- House veiled chameleons in a well-ventilated cage with a fine ($^1/_8$-inch or .3-cm) screen for sides or for an all-screen top.
- Use no substrate, only plain plastic or glass as cage flooring, because otherwise the food will hide and the chameleon's tongue will pick up debris, which can cause intestinal blockage.
- Provide light and heat by means of a 30-to-50-watt reflector spot in a reflector hood.
- Exposure to direct ultraviolet light is highly beneficial; the sun is the chameleon's best source of light.
- Low cage limbs must be covered with artificial (silk or plastic) leaves to provide shelter.

- Do not allow your veiled chameleons to hang upside down from their cage top, as they can easily burn themselves, and they won't come down to feed and drink.
- Deliver water via one or two ice cubes placed on the screen top, with a wide shallow container (such as a plastic jar lid or a small food-storage container) on the enclosure floor below.
- Keep the cage bottom dry 23 hours a day.
- The day temperature (in the hottest spot) should be 95 to 110° F (35 to 43.3° C). The nighttime temperature should be 70 to 75° F (21.1 to 23.9° C) when the lights are off.
- Do not clean or rearrange cage furniture because this causes the veiled chameleon great stress.
- Veiled chameleons can be housed outdoors, above 58° F (14.4° C) at night, from April through October in fine-screen caging with a bare-ground bottom and live plants. Give the chameleons morning sun.

Food

Feed your hatchlings two-week-old crickets, offering them twice a day if possible. (Other types of food items are often regurgitated until the young are more than 7 inches or 17.8 cm in total length.) Be sure to "dust" all food items with a vitamin and mineral supplement rich in calcium and vitamin D_3 (Super Preen®, Nekton Rep®, Reptivite®, and Herptivite® are good choices) at every feeding by placing the food items in a tall, narrow container with a light amount of vitamin and mineral powder. Use a shaking motion to dust the insects with the supplement prior to offering them to your captives.

Note: Excessive amounts of vitamin D_3 may shorten the life or cause the premature death of adults. It is generally recommended that the amount of vitamin D_3 supplementation be reduced in the adult diet. When it is combined with regular exposure to sunlight, dietary vitamin D_3 can lead to calcification of internal organs.

It is absolutely essential to feed your insects a proper diet. Enriched chicken feed or Ziegler's Cricket Diet® are commonly used for captive-raised insects. And yes, adult "veils" eagerly eat plant material. Live ficus and pothos leaves are best offered indoors and acacia *(baileyana)*, a natural habitat and food source in the wild, is the best choice for outdoor caging systems. Wild-caught insects other than captive-raised crickets and king mealworms *(Zophobas)* are especially good for these chameleons.

Health Problems

Baytril® (enrofloxacin) is recommended for respiratory infections, which are usually caused by constant cool temperatures, inadequate cage ventilation, and/or very wet cage flooring. A minimum of two sides of your cage should be screened to provide adequate air movement. Dripping only two ice cubes into a shallow lid will prevent a soggy cage bottom while still providing enough water. Baytril® is best given orally for chameleons less than 7 inches (17.8 cm) in total length and should be injected in larger specimens. Consult your veterinarian for the exact dosage and recommended site of injection (the anterior portion of the body).

Oxytocin is not useful to induce egg-bound lizards, but small amounts (0.2 cc) of injectable calcium by a veterinarian may help a chameleon's fatigued or calcium-deficient muscles.

Eye problems can arise in a chameleon if you sprinkle vitamin powder from above in its presence.

Internal parasites are common, even in captive-bred veiled chameleons. Nematodes and coccidia are common and can be treated with drugs that are readily available from your veterinarian. Reptiles in your collection should be treated twice a year for protozoans and nematodes, even if no outward signs of stress are visible, as these parasites are easily transported by keepers and free-ranging insects.

The use of vitamin and mineral supplements cannot be over-emphasized, as soft bones can develop in only two weeks if the chameleon's nutritional regime is neglected.

Females that do not eat well immediately after egg laying are usually suffering from vitamin and mineral depletion. It is a good idea to give water-soluble vitamins two or three times daily and to assist the feeding by placing freshly killed food items into your animal's mouth at an upright angle.

Inadequate amounts of vitamin D_3 and respiratory infections are the two main killers of captive-bred calyptratus. Therefore, a well-ventilated outdoor cage, in warm weather, will eliminate 95 percent of all its health problems.

Growth and Reproduction

Chamaeleo calyptratus grows to a length of 8 to 13 inches or 20.3 to 33 cm (sexual maturity) in 5 to 6 months. During this period shedding occurs over several days (unlike *C. pardalis*), giving them a troubled or dry look, which is normal. This dead dry skin is then eaten by its owner, but if other chameleons are present they too will dine on these fragments, whether on or off their neighbor.

Mature females may lay every 90 to 120 days at a rate of 30 to 70 eggs per clutch, the record clutch being 86 eggs from an 8-month-old. House sexes both physically and visually apart except for mating. You should always introduce the female into the male's cage (not vice versa), being very careful not to agitate the male while doing so. A frightened male may attack and seriously injure a prospective mate. If the male is quickly rolling and unrolling his tail during such an introduction, he is threatening harm, so remove your female immediately.

A receptive female has blue spots along her back and casque and will not gape her mouth when approached by a courting male. Pairs that accept each other can be left together for 18 to 24 hours. From the moment of introduction you will see interaction between the couple, and actual mating frequently begins within 10 to 15 seconds!

Females turn from light green to a black body color with blue and yellow body spots, in the presence of a male, within 18 hours after a successful copulation. Because the female is receptive only for a 10-to-15-day period, the keeper should introduce pairs every 5 days. Unlike some species of chameleons, calyptratus does not fare well holding unfertilized eggs and may become eggbound if her calcium and vitamin D_3 levels are low.

Sperm storage for subsequent clutches is an active feature of the veils, and therefore no matings may be necessary for the next laying. Anytime you see blue spots on the back of a female you can test her with a male.

Egg laying occurs 20 to 30 days after a female's first copulation. Test your female by placing her in a 5-gallon (19-liter) bucket filled with only 4 to 5 inches (10.2 to 12.7 cm) of moist sand and kept at 82 to

90° F (27.8 to 32.2° C) via a 25-watt lightbulb placed in a hood directly over the bucket. If no digging begins within one hour, then return the chameleon to her home cage and try again the next day. Females will dig a tunnel with their front legs until they hit the bottom of the container, and laying has begun when you see the female turned around in the tunnel with her head facing outward.

The eggs are easily dug up, and no special care needs to be taken with regard to their movement or position at this stage. To prepare for incubation, use a one-pint plastic container of vermiculite or perlite at a rate of 1.5 parts medium to 1 part water by weight. Place 20 eggs per one-pint plastic container, such as a deli cup; leave 50 percent of each egg showing above the vermiculite, and punch two push-pin-size air holes in a clear lid. Check your eggs often and spray the insides of the container if the eggs form dents. Eggs take 144 to 230 days to hatch at a fluctuating temperature of 80 to 86° F (26.7 to 30° C) in the daytime and from 72 to 75° F (22.2 to 23.9° C) at night. After a laying you should place the female in her home cage and pay extra attention to feedings, so as to allow proper weight gain. A healthy female will take food within minutes after laying a clutch of eggs.

If a female retains fertile eggs and dies, you can remove her eggs from the oviduct, dry them with paper toweling, and successfully incubate them. Eggs removed from a veiled chameleon that was dead 17 hours still hatched healthy babies. When hatching time is imminent you will see some eggs begin to "sweat." This condensation sends a message (probably hormonal) that signals all the healthy babies to emerge simultaneously. Therefore, if you have a 60-egg clutch divided into three incubation cups, it is normal that all the neonates hatch in one cup before any other cup of siblings begins to hatch.

Your hatchlings will begin to feed within 2 to 3 days after hatching. How long will they live? That's up to each herpetoculturist's ability, but males should live between 4 and 8 years and females between 2 and 5 years, depending on their reproductive demands.

Conclusion

Chamaeleo calyptratus gives us as herpetoculturists a great chance for success, but the challenge for the keeper is a nutritional race. Captive-bred chameleons (females in particular) must be given contact with direct sunlight and fed insects that in turn have been fed a balanced diet and then powdered or dusted with a vitamin-mineral supplement. Otherwise, an egg-laying female will lose a nutritional step with each successive clutch laid, which can lead to egg-binding, weak hatchlings, and/or death. The potential of *calyptratus* is vast because of its size, vigor, and massive capacity for egg production. No other species offers us such an opportunity.

Part V

Parson's Chameleon
(Chamaeleo parsonii)
Natural History, Captive Management, and Breeding

by
Kenneth Kalisch

Latin name: *Chamaeleo parsonii* (Cuvier, 1824)
Common name: Parson's chameleon
Nominate form: *Chamaeleo parsonii parsonii* (Cuvier, 1824)
Subspecies: *Chamaeleo parsonii cristifer* (Methuen and Hewitt, 1913)

Originally described as *Cameleonis rariss* in 1768 by James Parsons and identified and named in honor of J. Parsons by G. Cuvier in 1824, Parson's Chameleon, *Chamaeleo parsonii parsonii*, is one of the largest Malagasy species of the Chamaeleonidae family.

Males have been recorded to a maximal size of 27.75 inches (69.5 cm) total length/16 inches (40 cm) snout-to-vent length and females 19.75 inches (49.5 cm)/11.75 inches (29.5 cm), respectively. There have been reports of males that exceeded the size of 29 inches total length (70 cm), which would supersede the size of the purported largest species, *Chamaeleo oustaleti*.

The coloration of the males is fairly stable with variations of green to turquoise-blue as the ground color with three brownish, slightly curved diagonal stripes that move down from the dorsum towards the anterior of the body. Highlighting the center of the flank is a pale yellow-white spot. (This spot varies in size and is sometimes completely absent from one side or both.) The eye turrets are large and can be a clear yellow to a deep copper/orange. Females are predominantly a uniform green varying from a yellow-green to a bluish-green. They share the same diagonal striping, although the stripes are much less pronounced. The center flank spot is also a variable. The squamation (scale arrangement) is homogeneous and smooth, formed of quadrangular scales. The male has a paired divergent rostral process, which is often verrucose (warty) and denticulated at its termination; the female has none. Both sexes have occipital lobes that appear as folds of approximately $\frac{1}{8}$ inch (3mm) at the posterior of the head. They possess no dorsal or ventral crest. Stress coloration in the males is a general blanching of overall color or a darkening, showing black diagonal stripes with dark spotting scattered over the body. Females that are stressed display an increase in yellow color, which shows as spots or blotches. When this coloration reaches its peak, the female appears to be yellow with green spotting.

The color variations of C. p. parsonii are more evident in the males. The common terms used to describe the variations are self-explanatory, for example, "yellow-lipped" and "green-eyed" forms. In the females the color variations are more subtle, usually confined to muted undertones of blue or yellow. These color variances most likely represent geographic differences.

The subspecies of C. parsonii, Chamaeleo parsonii cristifer, has some distinct differences from the nominate form. The subspecies is smaller, with males reaching a total length of 19 inches/10.5 inches snout-to-vent (47.5 cm/26 cm) and females 15.75 inches/8.75 inches (39.5 cm/22 cm). Both sexes have a dorsal crest that is distinct over the first half to two-thirds of the body, formed of small, regular, conical tubercles. Another distinguishing feature is a feeble parietal crest. Coloration of the males is variations of blue-green with a rust-orange blotch on the flanks. A pale yellow-white spot may be found in the center of each flank. Females are a green-brown with a rust-orange blotch on the flank and may also have the pale yellow-white spot.

Chamaeleo p. parsonii are usually found in the primary rainforest. Their range is predominantly in the montane forests of the elevated eastern zone of Madagascar. They are found from the north in Montagne d'Ambre to as far south as Fort Dauphin. They have also been found on the eastern island of Nosy Boraha as well as the northwestern island of Nosy Bé (possible locality of the "yellow-lipped" variation) and in Ambanja on the west coast of Madagascar. Rainfall is plentiful as well as variable, depending on localities. The east coast has the highest annual rainfall on the island (see chart on p. 113) Chamaeleo p. parsonii is most commonly found at altitudes of 1,300 to 4,000 feet (400 to 1,200 meters).

Chamaeleo p. cristifer is found in a limited range of the eastern zone of rainforest and does not overlap into the range of C. p. parsonii.

Figure 1. A close-up of the head of a female *Chamaeleo p. parsonii* in a captive environment. Photo by Ken Kalisch.

The sole location for this subspecies is Perinet (Andasibe). Rainfall is approximately 67 inches (170 cm) per year. It is found at altitudes of 2,600 to 4,200 feet (800 to 1,300 meters).

The habitat of *C. p. parsonii* and *C. p. cristifer*, for the most part, is confined to the eastern forest. The best way of understanding the environmental variations is to give an overview of the basic localities, physical range, and rainfall variations within the range of the *parsonii*, moving from north to south. The rainfall of Madagascar is heaviest in the eastern region, diminishing as it moves west, as well as from northern to southern localities. The temperature basically follows the same pattern. Coastline temperatures are the warmest, with the temperatures dropping as one moves east and with the increase in elevation (the temperature pattern reverts once past the high massif and temperatures start to increase as one moves into the western region of the island). The humidity is high, varying from 75 to 95 percent, depending on the time of year and rainfall, which on the east coast is fairly constant.

The physical and vegetative environment that the *parsonii* inhabit is divided into two basic types: the lowland evergreen and the high-altitude montane forests. The lowland forest canopy reaches approximately 100 feet (30 meters) and is noteworthy in that it is comprised of a very diverse tree population as well as ferns, palms, epiphytes, and bamboo. As one moves up in altitude and into the montane rainforest, the canopy lowers to around 65 to 80 feet (20 to 25 meters). The trees branch closer to their base in a more horizontal direction, thus creating fewer typical vertical trunks. There is an abundance of tree ferns, mosses, and lichens, as well as a large variety of fern species and impatiens. Whether or not the parsonii inhabit the original forest or areas of secondary growth is not known by the author. The fact that deforestation has left only 5 to 7 percent of the original forest surely threatens their range.

The behaviors of C. *parsonii* are remarkable in the sense that they are fairly sloth-like in their movements. Unlike most of the *Chamaeleo* species, which are fairly active throughout the day, the Parson's are sedentary for long periods. They will find a spot on a branch that suits them, and as long as water, food, and temperatures permit, commonly remain there for several days. If the preceding factors are constant, the lizard's main motivation for movement is defecation, usually once or twice per week. This activity consists of moving through their environment, defecating, and returning to the original roosting spot or choosing another.

The other obvious motive for an increase in the activity levels of the Parson's is to reproduce. The behavior exhibited in relationship to reproduction (especially significant in the male) is active for this species. The courtship is signaled by the male's intensification of coloration and the initiation of head nodding. The nodding consists of a rolling jerk, moving right to left. As the male approaches the female, the nodding continues. If the female is receptive, the male will mount her, and copulation occurs. The copulation can last from 10 to 30 minutes. If the female is not receptive, she will display yellow spotting, flatten her body laterally, extend the gular sac, and rock from side to side. When the males encounter each other they exhibit lateral flattening, gular extension, blanching of coloration, but no rocking motion. In place of the rocking behavior, males will straighten their legs, extend the tail out, raise it up over their back (see figure 2), and as the tail descends, roll it up. This display repeats as they approach each other. Like other *Chamaeleo* species, this is a ritual to establish or defend territory and/or reproductive rights. It is theorized that this behavior triggers the onset of reproduction. The males face off and may butt heads a few times. The end result is the retreat of the submissive or defeated male. It is extremely rare for them to cause physical harm to each other, but always use caution in new introductions.

With a basic understanding of their natural environment and behaviors, it is possible to apply this information to five areas of captive

SAMPLE EAST COAST LOCALES of *C. parsonii parsonii* and *C. parsonii cristifer*			
LOCATION	**ALTITUDES**	**ANNUAL RAINFALL**	**TEMPERATURE**
Montagne d' Ambre (north)	2,789 to 4,836 ft (850 - 1.474 m)	141+ inches (369 cm)	80° F (26° C) to 54° F (12° C)
Marojezy	2,600 to 4,750 ft (800 - 1,450 m)	118+ inches (300 cm)	84° F (29° C) to 59° F (15° C)
Perinet	2,600 to 4,625 ft (800 - 1,300 m)	67+ inches (170 cm)	73° F (23° C) to 37° F (2.8° C)
Ranomafana	2,625 to 3,937 ft (800 - 1200 m)	102+ inches (260 cm)	76° F (26° C) to 43° F (6.1° C)
Andringitra	2,300 to 5,000 ft (800 -1,500 m)	79+ inches (200 cm)	75° F (24° C) to 34° F (1.1° C)
Andohahela (south)	2,300 to 6,417 ft (800 - 1,956 m)	79+ inches (200 cm)	74° F (23° C) to 43° F (6.1° C)

care. (1) Size: This is a large species that needs a large environment in which it feels at ease. (2) Water: They come from regions with heavy rainfall and high humidity and need an abundant water supply. (3) Temperature: The regions that they frequent are cool; they need to be kept at temperatures below 85° F (29° C). (4) Light: They come from the higher elevations of deep forest and require indirect filtered light. (5) Food: Because of their size they prefer larger insect forms.

Using these five elements as guides, let's take each one and apply it to captive care. It is important to stress that these elements are interdependent. They are a man-made attempt to recreate, as closely as possible, the natural conditions in which the Parson's are found, in order to increase the likelihood of success in captive management.

Size

One of the more important aspects of captive care is the enclosure that the chameleon(s) will dwell in. The Parson's are a large species and in this regard will require a generous-size space. The minimum for a single lizard should be 3 feet wide by 3 feet long by 4 feet high (91 cm wide by 91 cm long by 30.5 cm high). The ideal medium to use for the enclosure is $\frac{1}{2}$-inch by 1-inch (1.3-cm by 2.5-cm) screening that is vinyl-coated (this protects the chameleons if they crawl on the screening). A single Parson's in the wild would inhabit a large territory, so provide them with as much cage space as possible. It is also important to place the cage at the proper height; the top should be around 6 feet (1.83 meters) from the ground.

The interior of the cage needs to contain an abundance of foliage and branches. The Parson's come from dense forest, so providing them with as much cover as possible will give them a better sense of security. This can be accomplished with the use of potted plants such as *Ficus benjamina. Schefflera arboricola,* and tree ferns, and hanging plants such as pothos, ivy, or other vining plants. The goal is to create an environment that provides them with privacy and security. The branches should be of the proper size and placed in predominantly horizontal modes. When choosing branches it is important for them to be of varying circumference with a textured surface to facilitate the chameleon's grip. Be sure that the branch circumference is slightly larger than the grip of their feet. The foliage and branches should not be so dense that the lizard's ability to navigate through the cage is impaired. There should be a balance of planting, with a lacework of branches, and within this, open areas.

Water

The environment the Parson's inhabit has an abundance of rainfall. This has a two-fold effect; high levels of humidity and a fairly consistent supply of drinking water. The Parson's are heavy, slow, and long drinkers. A thirsty Parson's can drink for as long as 45 minutes [personal observation]. They should be provided with a watering device that provides a regular, slow drip. This can be accomplished in many ways. The simplest method is to place a container with a pinhole in the bottom of it on top of the cage. Depending on the size of the container and the hole it will supply a constant drip for as long as several hours.

The other means of supplying water can be as elaborate as a timer-misting-drip system that is set at intervals to mist and/or drip several times a day, or as simple as a combination of the previously mentioned

Figure 2. A male *Chamaeleo p. parsonii* displaying a typical defense posture with the tail raised above the back. This is seen when defending their territory and/or reproductive rights. Photo by Ken Kalisch.

drip container and misting the foliage in the cage with a spray bottle. Whatever the choice is, the lizards will need to be given a fairly substantial amount of water on a daily basis. The goal is to provide water for drinking and humidity, but the environment should dry out between applications of water. An ever-present supply of water or wetness can increase the growth of harmful bacteria and fungi, so monitor these levels carefully. A good practice is to supply the lizards with a drip container in the morning as well as to mist the foliage, and to mist the foliage again in the late afternoon or early evening. Unless your climate is unusually dry, this should be adequate. If the humidity is low, a relatively simple solution is to purchase a cool-air humidifier (available at drugstores for around $20), which will increase the humidity without overwatering the cage. The Parson's need to be provided with an environment that is a balance of drinking water and humidity with the awareness that too much moisture can cause problems.

Temperature

The Parson's come from an environment that has a much wider range of temperatures than one would expect. Because of the altitude and seasonal variance it can range from the low 40s° F (5.5° C) to the mid 80s° F (30° C) with the average temperature hovering around 73° F (23° C). As the east coast of Madagascar goes through its winter, the higher elevations (which are cooler to begin with) go through a significant drop. The Parson's respond to this by going into a dormant phase. The temperature reduction has a direct effect on their activity levels as well as on their feeding and drinking patterns. They will find a specific place on a branch and stay there, sometimes for weeks, moving occasionally for food or to defecate. During this time they may eat an occasional insect and their water intake is slowed. The cessation of the "dormancy" is determined by the increase in the temperature and the lizards' gradual return to normal levels of activity. Throughout the dormancy there should be no appreciable weight loss, which should be monitored by periodic weighings of the lizards. If there is a substantial change in weight, the temperature should be gradually increased and feeding should resume. In captivity it is extremely important to assure that the lizards are in optimum health and are well acclimated before attempting a cooling down. The first effort is to provide them with a comfortable temperature range from 68 to 80° F (20 to 27° C) before exposing them to lower temperatures. Acclimation of Parson's from the wild can take many months. The most common mistake is to keep them at higher temperatures, which can lead to problems because of their slow metabolism. Higher temperatures can stress their systems and result in respiratory problems or other complications. Similar problems occur in *Chamaeleo* from montane climates when they are kept at elevated temperatures. Allowing time for the lizard to adjust will be beneficial to their health and reproductivity in the long run.

Light

The *parsonii* are found deep in the cloud rainforest. They are not known as heliophilic in the traditional sense as are C. *pardalis*, which bask laterally. The Parson's will sun themselves for warmth, but it is uncommon for them to bask for extended periods of time; they typically inhabit areas within dense foliage. Their environment is high in humidity, with heavy amounts of rainfall and a fair amount of cloud cover. Taking these factors into consideration, they probably do not encounter an abundance of direct sun, and at best they get filtered sun. In an outdoor cage it is important to provide them with a number of shaded spaces. Indoors, provide them with both incandescent and fluorescent light sources. The incandescent lights provide warming spots, as well as helping to dry the cage out between waterings; the fluorescent lights provide light for the lizards and have the additional benefit of assisting plant growth. The fluorescent lighting should be the main source of light, creating the appropriate levels of brightness without increasing temperature.

Figure 3. A female Parson's chameleon in an outdoor vivarium. Photo by Ken Kalisch.

The difficulty of creating a balance of the four preceding elements of husbandry is the challenge. The objective is creating a sizable, well-planted environment with the proper amount of humidity, water, light, and acceptable temperatures.

Food

The fifth element may seem an odd inclusion in regards to the care of Parson's, yet it is this author's opinion that it is equally important. Because of the Parson's size, food types and resources need to be explored. The most common foods in their natural environment are grasshoppers, butterflies, cockroaches, mantids, stick insects, moths, and assorted flies. There have been reports of adult Parson's occasionally eating small birds. Providing this food list in captivity would be fairly intimidating. Nevertheless, it is possible to provide them with a varied diet of insects. This means that herpetologists will need to expand their duties to include entomology and begin propagating insects. There are several species of cockroaches that are easy to culture. The two most commonly available species, *Blaberus craniiferus* and *Gramphadorhina porrtentosa* (hissing cockroach) are hardy and excellent large food sources. *Blaberus spp.*, being the more prolific of the two, would be an excellent starting point. The other commercially available insects are: crickets, superworms, butterworms, waxworms, and mealworms. The nutritional value of most of these insects can be improved through nutrient loading by feeding them rolled oats, ground legumes, corn meal, fresh greens, carrots, sweet potatoes, apples, and oranges. Additional insect supplementation can be provided by collecting grasshoppers, butterflies, moths, and snails from the wild, as long as it is done in areas that are free of pesticides. The key to the Parson's diet is diversity; offer these chameleons as diverse a diet as possible and nutrient-load the insects before offering them as food.

Personal Observations on Husbandry, Reproduction, Incubation, and Hatching

At this point the author will shift to a narrative of experiences with his captive care of Chamaeleo p. parsonii. *They have been in the author's care for four and a half years.*

The Parson's were purchased as newly imported young adults in late October 1991. The male was approximately 18 inches (45 cm) total length and weighed 234 grams (8.2 oz). The female was 14 inches (35 cm) total length and weighed 225 grams (7.9 oz). The pair were placed in an indoor cage 3 feet (.9 m) wide by 4 feet (1.2 m) long by 6 feet (1.8 m) high. The interior of the cage had several large *Ficus* trees, *Schefflera* trees, hanging vines, and a network of branches. The lighting consisted of two incandescent spots and a pair of 48-inch (1.2-m) double fluorescent fixtures. Each fixture contained one plant light and one Vita-Lite®. The lizards slowly adapted to their environment, eventually establishing their own specific perching and sleeping spots. The cage had a drip-cup system and was misted twice a day, morning and evening.

The Parson's seemed to drink regularly, but my initial concern was their lack of food intake. I offered them everything I had on hand—crickets, waxworms, mealworms, and butterworms—but they showed little interest. The next step was to procure other insect forms, and *Blaberus* were found and offered. The response was excellent, and both chameleons fed well, but my dilemma was the cost and availability of the cockroaches. I then began to collect wild cabbage moths and these became a favorite food but again were a limited resource. A source of grasshoppers was finally found and although somewhat costly, they were regularly available. With the food situation under control, the lizards' acclimation seemed to progress very well. In the next six months, they began to expand their diet to include a much wider variety of common insects. By May 1992, the weight of the male had increased by 185 grams (6.5 oz) and the female by 145 grams (5.1 oz).

Figure 4. Breeding behavior of the *Chamaeleo p. parsonii.* Photo by P. Skoog.

At this point, everything appeared to be stable. The lizards had been checked by a veterinarian and were clean of parasites. The adjustment to captivity appeared positive. Their activity levels were fairly sedentary compared to other species I had previously worked with, but I finally relaxed and accepted this as typical behavior. In March 1992, I observed the male showing interest in breeding, and activity levels of the pair seemed to increase. The male began to pursue the female, nodding and attempting to approach her, but the female seemed indifferent. When the male approached her she would move out of his reach but not much farther. I observed many attempts by the male to mount the female but observed no copulation.

In May 1992, the pair were moved to a 4 feet (1.2 m) wide by 8 feet (2.4 m) long by 7 feet (2.1 m) high outdoor enclosure with an earthen floor (the cage bottom was built into the ground) with planting and branch arrangements similar to the indoor cage. The cage had a drip system that was turned on daily for 30 to 45 minutes. The adjustment to the outdoor enclosure was easily made by both lizards. The temperatures ranged from 68 to 80° F (20 to 27° C). Over the next few weeks the pattern of behavior for the pair appeared normal. During this time, the breeding displays by the male seemed to gradually subside and the pair cohabited without incident. The male frequented the upper branches and the female usually occupied the mid-area of the cage.

Figure 5. *Chamaeleo p. parsonii* during oviposition. Photo by P. Choo.

In mid-June the female's food intake slowed and continued to diminish to an insect or two each week by mid-July. I began to think that her health might be compromised, although she showed no visible signs of illness or stress. The first step of my investigation was to weigh her, and the results were not what I had expected. Her weight was several grams higher than the previous weighing, even though she had been eating poorly. I also checked her for respiratory problems and parasites, but neither was present. I concluded at this point that she was in good health and simply going through a diminished eating phase. As mid-August approached, she started to show signs of weight loss. I decided to remove the male to a cage out of her view in order to determine if his presence caused her lack of interest in feeding, but she did not resume feeding. The last week of August 1992, the female became restless, moving about the cage, crawling on the sides, and showing signs of stress. Her coloration showed more yellow, especially on the eye turrets. On August 27th, I entered the cage to do my routine cleaning and found three eggs on the dirt floor. It was now clear what had been the cause of the female's appetite loss.

Two sides of the cage were covered with shade cloth to provide more privacy because the cage was in partial view of other species of *Chamaeleo*. I placed an additional 6 cubic feet (0.2 cubic meters) of potting soil onto the cage bottom to provide a more acceptable medium for the female to dig a nesting site. The following day I found three more eggs on the bottom of the cage. The female was continuing her movement through the cage but made no attempt to dig. Another day passed, with no additional eggs and no indication of digging. On the fourth day, the female was moved to the indoor cage she originally inhabited and was given an intramuscular injection (in the shoulder) at 11:30 a.m. of .03 mg of oxytocin. The female positioned herself on a branch midpoint in the cage. At 12:25 p.m., she began to show signs of discomfort and took on a crouching stance with her vent averted to the side and her tail coiled around the branch. An egg appeared at 12:45 p.m., and as the process of egglaying (dropping) went on, she moved slowly through the lower and mid-sections of the cage, maintaining a stationary position for a few minutes prior to oviposition. The eggs were released approximately every 15 to 25 minutes for a total of 29 eggs after labor was induced, bringing the total number of eggs to 35.

The female appeared thin. Her pre-oviposition weight was 325 grams (11.4 oz) and her post-gravid weight was 253 grams (8.9 oz), putting her total weight loss at 117 grams (3.9 oz) from her pregravid weight of 370 grams, 68 grams (2.2 oz) of the weight being eggs. Her food intake resumed slowly two days after oviposition and within two months she had regained 50 percent of her lost weight and seemed to recover fully.

The eggs appeared white with a surface texture not unlike the Parson's skin, each weighing slightly under 2 grams (0.1 oz). They were divided into three groups and placed in Tupperware® containers (see figure 5), the lids of which had approximately a dozen pinhole-size perforations. The substrate used in the containers was varied to ascertain whether the eggs would develop differently in different media. Two containers had a mixture of 80 percent vermiculite and 20 percent sterile soil; the third container had 80 percent sterile soil and 20 percent vermiculite. The question of how to properly incubate the eggs required some thought. Realizing that the adults are exposed to a wide range of temperatures and a dormant period, it was a fair assumption that the eggs would diapause, and the length of incubation had not been determined. Drawing from the limited information available and communications with colleagues, I decided to incubate the eggs for the first three months at approximately 74° F (23.3° C). The next three months the eggs would be subjected to a temperature of 65° F (18° C). After that, the temperature would be slowly increased to 74° F (23.3° C) over several weeks.

During the first three months the development of the eggs was nominal. Five of the eggs became moldy; upon opening them I found no indications of fertility (these were the eggs found in the outside cage). In the process of opening the eggs I discovered that the shell thickness of the egg was almost twice that of other *Chamaeleo* eggs. In mid-December another egg molded and showed no signs of development. As the incubation continued, the eggs were candled for signs of vascularization and appeared clear yellow, but I realized that candling would be somewhat limited because of the shell thickness. Over the next six months, the remaining eggs increased in size by 10 percent. The egg development between the two substrates showed no significant difference. The eggs were candled once a month, and while there was no clear indication of vascularization, there was a change in the color in

Figure 6. Incubation of *Chamaeleo p. parsonii* eggs. Photo by Ken Kalisch.

the seventh month to a reddish-orange. The temperature was maintained primarily at 74° F (24° C), and although the eggs were exposed to higher temperatures throughout the summer, they never exceeded 80° F (26.7° C). At the one year mark, the egg size had increased by 20 percent. Candling indicated further embryonic development, but again, due to shell thickness, it was unclear as to how far the development had progressed.

In October of 1993 one egg had a wet appearance. After several days the egg began to shrink and discolor. The egg was opened and inside was a solid yolk and an embryo approximately $\frac{1}{8}$ inch long within the yolk mass. Over the next four months, three more eggs repeated the same sequence, but inside the eggs were embryos of increasing size. The embryonic development was in the later stages, the largest embryo being close to $1\frac{1}{2}$ inches.

The eggs were put through a second cool-down period of three months from November 1993 to January 1994 at the same temperature as the first cool-down. Though all the substrate had been kept at the same level of moisture, the eggs in the container with the higher soil content started to develop differently. As the eggs began to increase in size they developed what appeared to be stretch marks, the outer layer of the eggshell separating in irregular splits. The eggs in the other containers did not show this development. I wondered if this splitting acted as a means of reducing the thickness of the sggshell to facilitate the embryo's emergence. In April 1994, the eggs were into the 21st month of incubation. On April 25th, one egg had a single slit but was not preceded by signs of typical sweating. By the 26th, there were two more slits, but no further development. On April 29th the egg was opened and inside was a fully formed neonate. It was alive but showed no signs of movement except for the tail when it was touched; this neonate died 5 days later. On the 29th another egg was found with a single slit, and again there was no further development. On June 1st this egg was opened and another fully formed neonate was found, but it was not living.

The eggs were checked for signs of hatching on the evening of June 4th and none was found. On the morning of the 5th a third egg had seven slits in a starburst pattern at the end, and by 4 p.m. the neonate emerged. The neonate weighed 2.4 grams (0.08 oz) and was $3\frac{1}{4}$ inches (8.3 cm) in total length. Its coloration was an overall brown with a cream stripe running down the ridge of the dorsum. The neonate was placed into a well-planted fine-screen cage.

In the last few weeks of the month, most of the remaining eggs continued to go through a disappointing and repeating pattern. The eggs would slit once with no further activity or they would reduce in size and start to discolor. Examination of the eggs showed fully developed embryos, although none were living. The zigzag stretchmark patterns on some of the eggs may have been caused by excessive moisture. Two of these eggs appeared to have ruptured, both containing fully formed neonates. Of the four eggs remaining at the time of this publication, one had slit and the neonate had partially emerged.

On July 5, twenty-three months from oviposition, a second hatchling emerged. This neonate was significant in that it showed the typical white spot on each flank; otherwise it was identical to the first. None of the remaining few eggs hatched; upon opening these eggs, full-term, dead neonates were found.

The growth of the two neonates was remarkable. They shed at six weeks of age and doubled their weight in the first two months. At six months they weighed 16.5 and 20 grams, with a total length of 7 and 9 inches, respectively. At seven months, the largest of the two appears to show the emergence of a rostral process, probably indicating that it is a male.

The low hatch rate of this clutch is as perplexing as it is unfortunate, yet this often occurs in other *Chamaeleo* species. It is this author's belief that it involved the incubation temperatures being too high, or

Figure 7. A six-week-old captive-bred *Chamaeleo p. parsonii.* Photo by Ken Kalisch.

possibly that the cool-down temperatures were not low enough. Research by Dr. Larry Talent suggests that a vitamin A deficiency may result in a weakening of the neonates, preventing successful emergence. The areas of incubation temperature ranges and the dietary requirements of adult Parson's need further exploration.

The adult pair of *C. parsonii* have continued to do well, going through a second dormant phase in the winter of 1992–93. Breeding behavior was observed in the spring of 1993, and the following September the female produced a second clutch of 40 eggs. The following year (1994–95) the same regime produced a third clutch of 29 eggs. The second clutch is presently incubating in 100 percent vermiculite substrate and have gone through a similar incubation

Conclusions

While this is not intended as a definitive guideline, I hope that this author has provided some basic aspects of captive care, reproduction, incubation, and hatching for *C. parsonii parsonii.* Because of their size and large cage requirements, they may not be an ideal choice for everyone, but these gentle "giants" are well worth the effort to continue research into their husbandry.

Acknowledgements

The author would like to express his gratitude to Todd Risley, Dorothy Kalisch, Ardi Abate, and Dawn Griffith for their support, knowledge, and patience. Without their participation, much of this work would not have been possible.
—Ken Kalisch, 1994

Literature Cited

Albignec, R., A. Jolly, and P. Oberle. 1984. *Key Environments, Madagascar*. Pergamon Press.

Brygoo, E.R. 1971. *Reptiles Sauriens Chamaeleonidae. Genre Chamaeleo. Faune de Madagascar*. 33: 223–40. Paris: Orston et CNRS.

Buckley, R. 1991. "Experiments with Habitat Trees," *The Vivarium*, Vol. 3, No. 3:10–30.

Castle, E. 1990. "Captive Reproduction and Neonate Husbandry of the Oustalet's Chameleon, *C. oustaleti*, at the Oklahoma City Zoological Park." (Fourteenth International Herpetological Symposium on Captive Propagation and Husbandry), pp, 25–34.

De Vosjoli, P. 1990. *The General Care and Maintenance of the True Chameleons, Part II*. Lakeside, CA: Advanced Vivarium Systems.

Glaw, F., and M. Vences. 1993. *A Field Guide to the Amphibians and Reptiles of Madagascar*. Privately published.

Great Britain Meteorological Office, Met. 0.617d, Tables of Temperature, Relative Humidity and Precipitation for the World, Part IV, Africa, the Atlantic Ocean South of 35° N and the Indian Ocean.

Henkel, F.W., and S. Heinecke. 1993. *Chameleons im Terrarium*. Hannover: Landbuch Verlag.

Parcher, S.R. 1974. "Observations on the Natural Histories of Six Malagasy Chamaeleontidae." Zeitschrift fur Tierspychol. 34:500–523.

Preston-Mafham, K. 1991. *Madagascar: A Natural History*. Facts on File, Inc.

Index